CHOCOLATE

JENNIE REEKIE

CHOCOLATE

Exeter Books

NEW YORK

First published in USA 1986
by Exeter Books
Distributed by Bookthrift
Exeter is a trademark of Bookthrift Marketing, Inc.
Bookthrift is a registered trademark of Bookthrift Marketing, Inc.
New York, New York

ISBN 0-671-08322-8

Printed in Portugal

CONTENTS

Acknowledgements
Food photography   Peter Myers
Home economist   Jackie Burrow
Stylist   Alison Williams

The author and publisher would also like to thank
The Glasshouse and Way-In Living, Harrods for kindly
loaning equipment for photography.

INTRODUCTION

Chocolate – an emotive word which immediately conjures up different images for different people. Some think immediately of a box filled with candies, such as rich, creamy truffles, others of a delicious, dark chocolate cake, like Sacher Torte or Devil's Food Cake, and then there are those whose mind immediately hones in on what many consider to be the king or queen of desserts – a superb chocolate mousse. No matter which of these is your favorite, all are included in this book together with more economical and simpler creations, many of which have a strong appeal to children who adore anything 'chocolatey'.

It is interesting to note that the Western love of chocolate is comparatively recent. Although it first came to Britain in the seventeenth century, it was really not until the middle of the nineteenth century, that it was regarded as anything other than a drink. This was partly because no-one had successfully mastered the art of producing anything other than chocolate 'nibs' (ie roasted and chopped cocoa beans) which are far from being a gourmet's delight, and partly because there was, until 1853, a prohibitive tax on cocoa beans.

The Aztec Indians in South America were the first known chocolate drinkers in the world, and it was here that a Spanish explorer in 1519 found their Emperor, Montezuma, drinking a pungent mixture called 'chocolatl' out of gold cups. It is said that the Emperor rationed himself to a mere 50 cups a day! One can only imagine that he was using it as a stimulant, bearing in mind that the cocoa beans contain small amounts of theorbromine, which has similar properties to caffeine.

Despite or because of these origins, chocolate rapidly developed its uses until it became what is probably the most popular sweet flavor in the Western world. Indeed, it is in its great versatility that chocolate finds such favor with the cook, whether as a warming drink on a cold winter's day, a luscious chocolate cake or dessert or as ice cream. Some truly wonderful masterpieces can be created without great skill and all will be acclaimed with great enthusiasm, simply because they are made with chocolate.

TYPES OF CHOCOLATE

There are three principal types of chocolate commonly used in cooking – unsweetened, couverture and semisweet or bittersweet chocolate, of which unsweetened chocolate is the one most frequently used in this book. White chocolate is not suitable for cooking because it contains no cocoa and, therefore, of course, no color.

Unsweetened chocolate is chocolate especially prepared for cooking. It enables you to achieve a strong chocolate flavor without the end result being too sweet, but I have restricted its use here to just one recipe as it is not very easy to obtain.

If you do find some, and want to experiment, try using it in one of your favorite recipes. It is particularly good in chocolate sauces or for baking – but remember to use slightly less of it than other chocolate and to add a little sugar.

Semisweet or bittersweet chocolate gives a good strong chocolate flavor. There are a number of different brands available; and some supermarkets have their own brands as well. Remember though that chocolate quality varies considerably. In order to be called chocolate, the product must have a minimum of 34 per cent cocoa solids. Some have as much as 47 per cent, so it is worth looking on the back of the package to check this.

As well as bars of chocolate, you can also buy packages of 'chips'. These have two particularly useful functions: they are good for melting chocolate because the small pieces melt quickly, and the size is perfect for making ice creams and cookies.

Milk chocolate is rarely used in cooking as it does not give a strong enough chocolate flavor. This can sometimes be an advantage if, for example, you wish to grate a small amount of chocolate over fruit with a delicate flavor. It is, however, used for making Easter eggs, chocolates and chocolate cases, such as the Apricot Fruit Basket on page 51.

Chocolate chips are probably the best thing to buy if milk chocolate is required for anything other than grating, as they are usually cheaper than bars.

Compound chocolate comes both sweetened and semisweet. It is not really chocolate because it does not have the required minimum of cocoa solids and contains added vegetable oil. It produces less flavor than semisweet chocolate, but has some advantages. It is cheaper and easier to melt than semisweet chocolate. It also avoids the streaky effect sometimes visible after melted semisweet chocolate has set.

Cocoa is certainly the cheapest, and sometimes the best, way of obtaining a good, strong chocolate flavor, especially when baking. However, it is not used as extensively as unsweetened chocolate for desserts and mousses where a richer flavor is required.

Instant chocolate milk mix can be used to give a more subtle flavor, but as it is very sweet it is almost always necessary to reduce the amount of sugar in the recipe.

Basic
Information

Making Chocolate Decorations

Chocolate can be used to make a variety of extremely attractive decorations. These can be used on all kinds of cakes, puddings and desserts, quite apart from chocolate ones. For example, cream-topped trifles and pale iced cakes make a perfect foil for the dark appeal of chocolate.

For most decorations the chocolate must be melted and the finished product allowed to set quite hard. This should not be done in a refrigerator or the chocolate will acquire an unattractive chalky 'bloom'. It is best to leave it in the coolest, driest place you have – I put mine, covered, in a shady corner of the back yard when the season permits (a kitchen is too warm and steamy to be suitable).

Above *Making chocolate horns (page 10)*

Below *Making caraque (page 10)*

Below *Making chocolate leaves (page 10)*

Grated chocolate is the simplest and quickest of decorations, and is very effective. Using a metal grater, and making sure that your hands are cool, grate the chocolate directly on to the food or, if you prefer, on to a plate from where it can be sprinkled with a metal spoon. Do not use your fingers to work with the grated chocolate as the fine particles will melt quickly.

Chocolate curls can be made from semisweet or couverture chocolate. Use a thick bar of chocolate – the thicker the bar the more successful the results – and make sure it is at the right temperature, ie if it is too cold and hard the chocolate will break; if it is too warm and soft the curls will not hold their shape. Simply scrape a vegetable peeler over the back of the bar of chocolate and roll the curls on to a plate. Lift them from the plate with the point of a sharp knife on to the surface to be decorated.

Caraque are long chocolate curls which give a professional and rather glamorous finish to many cakes and gâteaux. Melt the chocolate (page 10) and spread it with a spatula to less than ¼ inch thick over an ungreased surface, preferably a Formica counter or a marble slab. Leave to set in a thin layer. Holding the blade of a knife at an angle of 45°, push away from you and scrape off long curls. Lift them carefully, as they are fragile, using the point of the knife or a skewer; do not discard the small flakes of chocolate that remain on the working surface after you have finished; they can be scattered on top of the cake or dessert in between the pieces of caraque.

Chocolate leaves are made by using real fresh leaves as a mold. The most commonly used leaves are rose leaves because they have a pleasing shape and prominent veining which impresses itself on the chocolate and glossy finish which makes them easy to work with. Any leaves will do, however, as long as they are not poisonous.

Wash and dry the leaves thoroughly. Dip the underside, which has the most prominent veins, into melted chocolate (page 10) to give a thick and even coating; alternatively, paint on the chocolate. Place on waxed or non-stick silicon paper to set. Let the chocolate set completely hard, then carefully peel off the leaf.

Horns are made with the help of cream horn tubes. Wash and dry them and shine the inside of the tubes with absorbent paper. Pour in some melted chocolate (page 10). Tilt and turn the tube so that the chocolate coats the inside evenly; repeat the process to obtain a thicker layer of chocolate (this will be easier to unmold. As you become more proficient, you can make thinner horns.) Leave to set in a cool, dry place. When the chocolate is completely hard, and has begun to shrink away from the inside of the tube, carefully ease out the chocolate horn with the point of a knife.

Chocolate animals are also made by pouring melted chocolate (page 10) into molds; these are available from good gourmet shops and are the perfect decoration for children's party cakes.

Shapes, patterns and designs can be made in two ways:
(1) Pencil your chosen design lightly on a piece of waxed or non-stick silicon paper. Melt the chocolate (page 10) and pour it into a pastry bag or nylon piping bag fitted with a small writing pipe. Follow the outline of your drawing first, and fill in the shape afterwards. If you are not making a solid design, but are tracing a trelliswork pattern, for example, make sure that you join up all the threads of chocolate, or the finished design will crack easily when you pick it up after it has set.
(2) Melt the chocolate (page 10) and spread in a thin layer with a spatula on a piece of wax or non-stick silicon paper. Leave to set. When the chocolate is hard, but not brittle, use cookie cutters or a sharp knife to cut out the shapes you want. You can buy cutters in all shapes, from crescents, hearts and bells to butterflies and stars. Simple shapes like squares and triangles can, of course, be cut out with a sharp knife and a steady hand!

Drizzled chocolate is a simple but extremely effective method of decorating cakes, ice cream or cookies. Simply melt the chocolate in a polythene bag, snip off a corner of the bag and let the chocolate drip over the food to be decorated.

Tips on Using Chocolate

MELTING CHOCOLATE

The way in which you melt chocolate is extremely important so as to avoid a solid mass with which you can do nothing.

Break the chocolate into pieces (or use chocolate chips) and put into a bowl over a pan of hot, not quite simmering, water (it must *not* be rapidly boiling). If using an electric cooker, turn off the heat once the water has boiled and leave the pan on the ring. Make sure that the bowl fits comfortably into the pan so that neither steam nor boiling water get into the bowl. As soon as the chocolate has melted, remove from the heat and use as required.

If, you do, however, end up with a solid mass, it is sometimes possible to rectify this by adding a little vegetable oil and beating it well. This works for mousses and similar desserts but not for decorations where it is important for the chocolate to set hard.

Chocolate can also be melted with the addition of solid vegetable oil. This makes it more liquid and easier to handle.

If you are only melting a small quantity of chocolate, such as 1 oz, you may find it easier to put the chocolate into a polythene bag, then to seal it and stand the bag in hot, *not* boiling, water. It is important to use a heavy gauge polythene and to ensure that there are no small holes in the bag.

Melting chocolate in a bowl in a slow oven is an alternative method recommended by some manufacturers.

A microwave oven can also be used for this purpose. Put the chocolate broken into pieces, in a suitable bowl, cover with clingfilm and place in the oven. The exact time it takes to melt the chocolate depends on the quantity, the size of the bowl, etc.

PREPARING CHOCOLATE FOR DIPPING

When using chocolate for dipping, ie for fresh fruit or for chocolates, you may find the chocolate a little easier to use if you add 1 tablespoon vegetable oil or 1 tablespoon white vegetable shortening to every 6 oz chocolate.

Melt the chocolate, then pour it into a small jar or glass wide and deep enough for the fruit or chocolate to be dipped into and totally covered.

Hold the ingredient to be dipped with a special dipping fork, fondue fork, skewer or toothpick. Dip into the melted chocolate, allow the excess to run off, then remove the dipped ingredient from its fork by pushing it off gently with another fork, skewer or toothpick.

MAKING 'BITTER' CHOCOLATE

As unsweetened chocolate is not easy to find, semisweet chocolate is generally substituted. Where this is a little too sweet for certain recipes, the chocolate can be made slightly 'bitter' by adding either 1 teaspoon instant coffee powder or granules, or a little very strong black coffee. Alternatively, 1 teaspoon cocoa powder can be added for every 2 oz chocolate.

GRATING CHOCOLATE

During hot weather it is best to put the chocolate in a refrigerator for about 30 minutes before grating. If your hands are rather hot, hold the chocolate in a piece of paper toweling when grating.

CHOPPING CHOCOLATE

This can be done very successfully in a food processor and for many recipes this gives a very good size of chocolate chip. It is not, however, easy to chop chocolate manually, and it is better, in this case, to grate it coarsely.

USING COCOA AND INSTANT CHOCOLATE MILK MIX

When baking, sift cocoa and instant chocolate milk mix with other dry ingredients so that any lumps are removed.

If using cocoa in buttercream, etc, it is important to cook the starch in it, so it should be blended with *very hot* water. (Do not use boiling water as it tends to make a solid lump which is difficult to use.)

OTHER POINTS

When using any kind of mold, ensure that it is scrupulously clean so that the chocolate does not stick to the mold and crack. Wash the mold thoroughly in warm water, then dry and polish with a piece of paper toweling.

Cakes, Gâteaux and Cookies

Baking is always considered to be one of the most satisfying forms of cooking; I still experience a little thrill when I open the oven door and see a beautifully risen cake which not long before was just a flat mixture in a pan. Make this into a chocolate cake and the pleasure is doubled because of the popularity of this somewhat addictive ingredient. Over the years, my children have always come back with 'a chocolate cake please' when asked which cake they wanted for their birthday – apart from one memorable occasion when there was a request for an orange cake.

Whilst I have not included any specific birthday cakes in this chapter, there are a number of cakes which would serve as a very good base, eg the Simple Cake on page 19 is very suitable for children as it is not too rich. Equally, many of the gâteaux would undoubtedly be very popular as birthday cakes for adults. Jill Van den Bosch who so painstakingly typed this manuscript for me made the Sacher Torte for her mother's birthday and tells me that it was greatly appreciated by everyone.

Although one can buy any number of excellent cookies, there is nothing quite like home-made cookies in the tin. They are a great standby, as most of them keep well in an airtight tin, or can be frozen and do not take long to defrost.

As well as making the recipes I have given here, you may like to coat one side of any of your favorite cookies with chocolate. This is a good way for young children to do some 'cooking' without making havoc. Melt some compound chocolate for them and let them spread it on shop cookies; they will keep quietly busy for ages, even if they do get a bit sticky!

As I prefer moist, rich chocolate cakes I have not included many small cakes; these have a tendency to dryness and can be very fiddly to frost and decorate. An exception is Cherry Fingers on page 30 which have the essential qualities of moistness and richness.

Chocolate and Orange Cake

2 cups self-rising flour
$\frac{3}{4}$ cup cocoa powder
1 cup unsalted butter
$1\frac{1}{4}$ cups caster sugar
2 eggs, beaten
1 cup buttermilk

FILLING AND FROSTING
1 cup unsalted butter
grated rind of 1 orange
2 cups confectioners sugar, sifted
juice of $\frac{1}{2}$ orange

DECORATION
fresh orange sections

Grease and line two 8–9 inch layer-cake pans. Sift together the flour and cocoa. Cream the butter and sugar until light and fluffy, then gradually beat in the eggs. Stir in the buttermilk. Fold in the flour and cocoa.

Turn the mixture into the prepared pans and bake in a medium oven, 350°F for about 40 minutes. Remove from the oven and allow to cool in the pans for 5 minutes. Turn out on to a wire rack and leave to cool. When cold, split each cake into two layers.

To make the frosting, cream the butter with the orange rind until soft. Gradually beat in the confectioners sugar, alternately with the orange juice. Use some of the buttercream to sandwich the cakes together. Spread the remaining buttercream over the top and sides of the cake, and mark with a fork. Decorate the top of the cake with the orange sections.

Cakes and Cookies
Chocolate and Orange Cake, Chocolate Ginger Squares (page 30), Florentines (page 33), Shortcake Zig-zags (page 37), Chocolate Meringues (page 34), Apple Cake (page 21) **and** *Spice Cake (page 18)*

Economical Chocolate Cake

¼ cup softened margarine
½ cup caster sugar
1 egg, beaten
1½ cups flour
a pinch of salt
2 teaspoons baking soda
1 tablespoon cocoa powder
4 tablespoons milk

FROSTING
¼ cup margarine
1 tablespoon cocoa powder
2½ cups confectioners sugar, sifted
2 tablespoons hot water

Grease and line a 7 inch baking pan. Cream the margarine, add the sugar and continue to beat until the mixture is light and fluffy. Beat in the egg, a little at a time. Sift together the flour, salt, baking soda and cocoa and fold into the creamed mixture, alternately with the milk.

Turn the mixture into the prepared pan and bake in a medium oven, 350°F, for about 50 minutes, or until the top springs back when pressed lightly. Allow to cool in the pan for 5 minutes, then turn out on to a wire rack and leave to cool. When the cake is quite cold, split into two rounds.

To make the frosting, put the margarine and cocoa into a small pan over low heat until the margarine has melted. Remove from the heat and beat in about a third of the confectioners sugar, then beat in a little of the hot water and the remaining confectioners sugar alternately. Beat well until the mixture begins to thicken. Spread evenly over both rounds, and swirl the frosting up on the top of the cake with a round-bladed knife or fork to make an attractive pattern. Sandwich the rounds together. Leave to set for at least 15 minutes.

Note It is particularly important that the margarine for the cake is very soft.

Wholewheat Chocolate Cake

¼ cup butter
¾ cup light soft brown sugar
2 tablespoons molasses
3 eggs, beaten
1 cup wholewheat flour
⅓ cup cocoa powder
2 teaspoons baking powder
2 tablespoons milk

FROSTING AND DECORATION
½ cup butter
⅔ cup soft brown sugar
5 tablespoons water
¼ cup cocoa powder
6 walnut halves

Grease and line an 8 inch baking pan. Cream together the butter, sugar and molasses until pale in color. Beat in the eggs, a little at a time, adding 1 tablespoon of the flour with the last amount of egg. Sift in the cocoa powder and baking soda, and fold in gently. Fold in the remaining flour and finally fold in the milk.

Turn the mixture into the prepared pan and bake in a medium oven, 350°F, for 1 hour or until the top springs back when pressed lightly. Remove from the oven, turn out on to a wire rack and leave to cool. When cold, split the cake into two rounds.

To make the frosting, put all the ingredients, apart from the walnuts, into a pan and stir over low heat until the sugar has dissolved. Boil rapidly for 2 minutes. Remove from the heat, and allow to cool slightly, stirring frequently. Spread 2 tablespoons of the frosting over the bottom round of cake. Sandwich the two cake rounds together. When the frosting is the consistency of light cream, pour the remainder over the cake to coat the top and sides. Decorate with the walnut halves and leave to set.

Dark Chocolate Cake

2½ oz flour
2 tablespoons cocoa powder
4 oz bitter chocolate, broken into pieces
3 tablespoons water
½ cup butter
½ cup **caster sugar**
4 eggs, separated

FILLING
6 tablespoons chocolate spread
3 tablespoons apricot jam, sieved
1 tablespoon water

FROSTING
1½ cups confectioners sugar
2 tablespoons cocoa powder
2 oz bitter chocolate
¼ cup butter
2 tablespoons milk

Grease and line an 8 inch round cake pan. Sift together the flour and cocoa. Melt the chocolate with the water (page 11). Remove from the heat and cool. Cream the butter and sugar until light and fluffy. Beat in the yolks, one at a time, beating well after adding each one. Fold in the flour alternately with the chocolate. Beat the whites until stiff, then fold in gently.

Turn the mixture into the prepared pan and bake in a moderate oven, 350°F, for about 50 minutes, or until the top springs back when pressed lightly. Allow to cool in the pan for a few minutes, then turn out on to a wire rack and leave to cool. When cold, split into three rounds.

Sandwich the rounds together with the chocolate spread. Put the jam and water in a small pan and bring to the boil. Boil for 1 minute. Use to brush the top and sides of the cake.

To make the frosting, sift together the confectioners sugar and cocoa. Melt the chocolate in a bowl with the butter and milk. Remove from the heat and beat in the sugar and cocoa to give a thick, glossy frosting. Spread the frosting over the cake at once, then leave in a cool place to set.

Moist Chocolate Cake

2½ cups soft brown sugar
¼ cup cocoa powder
½ cup water
2 cups flour
2 teaspoons baking soda
½ teaspoon bicarbonate of soda
½ teaspoon salt
½ cup butter
1 teaspoon vanilla extract
2 eggs, separated
½ cup sour cream

FILLING AND DECORATION
4 tablespoons chocolate
and hazelnut spread
confectioners sugar

Grease and line two 8 inch layer cake pans. Put ¾ cup of the sugar into a pan with the cocoa and water. Stir over low heat until the sugar has dissolved, then bring to the boil and simmer gently for 2 minutes. Remove from the heat and allow to cool. Sift together the flour with the baking soda, bicarbonate of soda and salt. Cream the remaining sugar and the butter until light and fluffy. Add the vanilla extract and beat in the egg yolks, one at a time. Fold in the dry ingredients alternately with, first, the cooled chocolate and then the sour cream. Beat the egg whites until stiff and fold gently into the mixture.

Turn the mixture into the prepared pans and bake in a medium oven, 350°F, for about 45 minutes or until the cakes spring back when pressed lightly. Allow to cool in the pans for 2 minutes, then turn out on to a wire rack and leave to cool.

When cold, sandwich the cakes together with the chocolate and hazelnut spread. Dust the top with confectioners sugar.

BANANA AND WALNUT CAKE

¾ cup butter
½ cup caster sugar
3 eggs, beaten
1½ cups self-rising flour
½ cup instant chocolate milk mix
½ cup walnuts, chopped finely

FILLING AND DECORATION
½ cup heavy cream
2 tablespoons milk
2 bananas
1 tablespoon lemon juice
¼ cup confectioners sugar, sifted
extra confectioners sugar

Grease and line two 7 inch layer-cake pans. Cream the butter and sugar together until light and fluffy. Gradually beat in the eggs, a little at a time, adding 1 tablespoon of the flour with the last amount of egg. Sift in the remaining flour and the instant chocolate milk mix, and fold into the mixture. Fold in the walnuts.

Turn the mixture into the prepared pans and bake in a moderately hot oven, 375°F, for about 25 minutes. Remove from the oven and allow to cool in the pans for a couple of minutes, then turn out on to a wire rack and leave to cool.

To make the filling, whip the cream with the milk until it is just stiff. Slice the bananas and toss in the lemon juice. Fold into the cream with the confectioners sugar. Sandwich the cakes together with the banana cream and dust the top with confectioners sugar before serving.

SACHER TORTE

8 oz semisweet chocolate, broken into pieces
1 tablespoon strong black coffee
1 cup butter
1 cup sugar
5 eggs, separated
1½ cups self-rising flour, sifted

FILLING
4 tablespoons apricot jam, sieved

FROSTING
6 oz semisweet chocolate, broken into pieces
5 tablespoons strong black coffee
1½ cups confectioners sugar, sifted

Grease and line a 9 inch cake pan. Melt the chocolate with the coffee (page 11) and allow to cool. Cream the butter and sugar until light and fluffy. Beat in the egg yolks, one at a time, then the cooled chocolate. Fold in the flour. Beat the egg whites until they form stiff peaks, then fold gently into the mixture.

Turn the mixture into the prepared pan and bake in a cool oven, 300°F, for 1½ hours. Leave to cool in the pan for 15 minutes, then turn out on to a wire rack and leave to cool. When quite cold, split the cake into two rounds.

To make the filling, warm the apricot jam gently. Spread one round of the cake with most of the apricot jam, sandwich the rounds together, then brush the remainder of the apricot jam all over the cake.

To make the frosting, melt the chocolate with the coffee (page 11). Remove from the heat and beat in the confectioners sugar. Pour the frosting over the cake, spreading it evenly with a spatula dipped in warm water. Leave to set for at least 1 hour. Serve with whipped cream.

Black Forest Gâteau (page 22), Sacher Torte **and** *Dobos Torte (page 27)*

SPICE CAKE

¼ cup butter
1½ cups caster sugar
4 eggs, separated
2 oz semisweet chocolate, broken into pieces
1 cup mashed potato
1¼ cups flour
½ teaspoon baking soda
2 teaspoons baking powder
½ teaspoon salt
1 teaspoon ground cinnamon
½ teaspoon ground nutmeg
½ teaspoon ground cloves
½ cup milk

Grease and flour a 3 lb loaf pan. Cream the butter and sugar until light and fluffy, then beat in the egg yolks. Melt the chocolate (page 11). If the potatoes are cold, heat in a non-stick skillet until lukewarm (any hotter and they will melt the butter). Beat the chocolate into the butter and sugar, then beat in the potatoes. Sift the flour with the baking soda, baking powder, salt and spices. Fold into the mixture alternately with the milk. Whisk the egg whites until stiff, then fold gently into the mixture.

Turn the mixture into the prepared pan and bake in a medium oven, 350°, for about 1¼ hours or until a skewer inserted into the center comes out clean. Allow to cool in the pan for 5 minutes, then turn out on to a wire rack and leave to cool. Serve sliced.

FUDGY DATE CAKE

¾ cup butter
½ cup soft brown sugar
2 tablespoons corn syrup
3 eggs, beaten
1¾ cups self-rising flour, sifted
⅓ cup dried dates, chopped
4 oz semisweet chocolate, grated coarsely
or chopped finely

Grease and line a 9 inch deep layer cake pan. Cream together the butter, sugar and syrup until light and fluffy. Beat in the eggs gradually, adding 1 tablespoon of the flour with the last amount of egg. Fold in the remainder of the flour, then fold in the dates and chocolate.

Turn the mixture into the prepared pan and bake in a medium oven, 350°F, for about 45 minutes. Turn out on to a wire rack and leave to cool.

Jewish Passover Chocolate Cake

½ cup butter
½ cup caster sugar
4 eggs, separated
1 cup ground almonds
¾ cup fine matzo meal
4 oz bitter chocolate, grated
grated rind of ½ orange
juice of 1 large orange

Grease and line an 8 inch cake pan. Cream the butter and sugar together until light and fluffy. Gradually beat in the egg yolks. Fold in the ground almonds, matzo meal, chocolate and orange rind and juice. Whip the egg whites until they form stiff peaks, then fold into the mixture.

Turn the mixture into the prepared pan and bake in a warm oven, 325°F, for about 50 minutes. Allow to cool in the pan for 2–3 minutes, then turn out on to a wire rack and leave to cool.

Simple Cake

1¼ cups self-rising flour
¼ cup cocoa powder
a pinch of salt
1 cup caster sugar
½ cup butter **or** margarine
¾ cup canned evaporated milk
2 eggs
2 tablespoons water
1 teaspoon vanilla essence

FILLING AND TOPPING
2 cups confectioners sugar
¼ cup cocoa powder
⅓ cup butter

Grease and line two 7½–8 inch layer-cake pans. Sift together the flour, cocoa, salt and sugar into a large bowl. Melt the butter or margarine in a pan. Take 3 tablespoons of the evaporated milk and put into a small pan for the frosting. Put to one side. Beat the eggs with the remaining evaporated milk, water and vanilla extract. Make a well in the center of the dry ingredients, add the egg mixture together with the melted fat, and beat well until blended.

Divide the mixture between the prepared pans and bake in a medium oven, 350°F, for 20–25 minutes or until the cakes spring back when pressed lightly. Allow to cool in the pans for a few minutes, then turn out on to a wire rack and leave to cool.

To make the filling, sift the confectioners sugar and cocoa into a bowl. Put the butter into the pan with the reserved milk, and heat gently until the butter has melted. Pour over the confectioners sugar mixture and beat until well blended. Put to one side for about 10 minutes until the mixture begins to thicken. Use some of the mixture to sandwich the cakes together, and spread the remaining frosting over the top and sides. Decorate as liked.

RUM CAKE

½ cup self-rising flour
½ teaspoon baking soda
6 tablespoons cocoa powder
3 tablespoons dark rum
6 tablespoons cold water
½ cup butter
1 cup caster sugar
2 eggs, beaten
½ cup ground almonds

Grease and line a 7½–8 inch round cake pan. Sift together the flour and baking soda. Sift the cocoa into a bowl and stir in the rum and water. Cream the butter and sugar until light and fluffy. Gradually beat in the eggs, a little at a time. Fold in the ground almonds gently, then the flour and cocoa mixture alternately.

Turn the mixture into the prepared pan and bake in a warm oven, 325°F, for about 1 hour or until the cake springs back when pressed lightly. Allow to cool in the pan for 5 minutes, then turn out on to a wire rack and leave to cool. Wrap in wax paper and foil, or store in an airtight tin until required.

Serve with plenty of whipped cream or Crème Chantilly (page 62).

Note This cake is best if kept for at least 24 hours before serving so that it becomes very soft and moist. Once cut, it should be eaten as soon as possible.

DEVIL'S FOOD CAKE

½ cup milk
1 cup soft brown sugar
1 cup cocoa powder
½ cup butter
2 eggs, beaten
2 cups flour
1 teaspoon bicarbonate of soda

FROSTING
2 cups granulated sugar
½ cup water
2 egg whites

Grease and line an 8 inch baking pan. Put the milk, sugar, cocoa and butter in a pan. Heat gently, stirring until melted and smooth. Leave to cool. Beat in the eggs until smooth. Sift together the flour with the bicarbonate of soda and beat into the chocolate mixture to give a smooth thick batter.

Pour the batter into the prepared pan and bake in a warm oven, 325°F, for about 1 hour until risen and firm. Allow to cool in the pan for 5 minutes, then turn out on to a wire rack and leave to cool. When cold, split into three rounds.

To make the frosting, put the sugar and water in a small pan. Stir over low heat to dissolve the sugar, then boil to 240°F on a candy thermometer (soft ball stage). Beat the egg whites in a large mixing bowl until very stiff. When the syrup has reached the required temperature, allow the bubbles to subside, then pour on to the beaten egg whites, beating all the time. Continue beating until the frosting thickens and stands in soft peaks. Use at once to sandwich together the rounds of cake. Spread the remaining frosting over the cake, swirling with a spatula and pulling up into peaks. Leave to set for 30 minutes.

APPLE CAKE

3 tart apples
juice of $\frac{1}{2}$ lemon
2 eggs
$\frac{3}{4}$ cup caster sugar
$\frac{1}{2}$ cup butter
$\frac{1}{2}$ cup milk
6 oz compound chocolate,
broken into pieces
$1\frac{3}{4}$ cups flour
3 teaspoons baking soda

Grease and flour an 8 × 12 inch roasting pan. Peel, core and slice the apples thinly. Put in a bowl of cold water with the lemon juice and put to one side. Beat the eggs with $\frac{2}{3}$ cup of the sugar until thick and creamy, and the beater leaves a trail when lifted out of the mixture.

Put the butter, milk and chocolate into a pan. Heat gently until the butter and chocolate have melted, then bring to the boil. While still boiling, pour the mixture over the eggs and sugar and stir until well blended. Sift in the flour and baking soda, and fold in carefully.

Turn the mixture into the prepared pan. Drain and dry the apple slices, and arrange them evenly over the top of the mixture (this is important – too much apple in the center and the edges will burn before the center has cooked). Sprinkle with the remaining sugar and bake in a moderately hot oven, 400°F, for about 30 minutes. Serve warm with cream, or cool in the pan, and serve sliced.

HONEY CAKE

1 cup honey
1 cup caster sugar
$\frac{1}{4}$ cup butter
$\frac{1}{2}$ cup ale
1 egg, beaten
3 cups flour
2 teaspoons baking soda
3 teaspoons ground allspice
1 cup ground almonds

FROSTING AND DECORATION
2 oz semisweet chocolate, broken into pieces
2 tablespoons hot water
2 tablespoons butter
1 cup confectioners sugar
$1\frac{1}{2}$ tablespoons cocoa powder
4 tablespoons apricot jam, sieved
$\frac{1}{2}$ cup blanched flaked almonds

Grease and line a 13 × 9 inch jelly roll pan. Put the honey, sugar, butter and ale in a large pan. Stir over low heat until the butter has melted and the sugar dissolved. Remove from the heat and allow to cool. Beat the egg into the mixture. Sift together the flour, baking soda and allspice, then beat gradually into the melted ingredients. Stir in the almonds.

Turn the mixture into the prepared pan and spread evenly. Bake in a moderately hot oven, 375°F, for about 20 minutes or until firm. Remove from the oven, and turn out of the pan on to a wire rack (the cake should be frosted while it is still warm).

To make the forsting, melt the chocolate with the water and butter (page 11), then remove from the heat. Sift in the confectioners sugar and cocoa and beat well. Replace the bowl over the hot water to keep the frosting warm. Warm the apricot jam in a small pan. Spread evenly over the top of the cake, then spread with the frosting. Arrange the flaked almonds on the top of the cake, then cut into squares. Serve warm, or leave to cool, and store in an airtight tin.

CHOCOLATE AND CHESTNUT LOG

¼ cup flour
¼ cup cornstarch
1½ tablespoons cocoa powder
1 teaspoon baking soda
3 eggs **plus** 1 egg white
¾ cup caster sugar
15 oz canned unsweetened chestnut purée
¼ cup soft brown sugar
2 tablespoons dark rum
2 oz semisweet chocolate
½ cup heavy cream
3 tablespoons light cream

Grease and line a 13×9 inch jelly roll pan. Sift together the flour, cornstarch, cocoa and baking soda. Beat the eggs with the extra egg white, in a large mixing bowl. Beat in the sugar, 1 tablespoon at a time. Continue to beat until the mixture is the consistency of very lightly whipped cream. Beat in the sifted ingredients, 1 tablespoon at a time; beat well after each addition.

Turn the mixture into the prepared pan, and spread evenly. Bake in a moderately hot oven, 400°F, for about 12 minutes or until the cake springs back when pressed lightly. Turn out on to a piece of wax or non-stick silicon paper, dredged with confectioners or caster sugar. Carefully peel off the lining paper, trim off the edges, and roll up the jelly roll, keeping the paper inside the roll. Put to one side and allow to cool.

To make the filling, beat the chestnut purée with the brown sugar and rum to give a soft spreading consistency. Grate the chocolate coarsely or form into curls with a vegetable peeler (page 10). Whip the heavy and light creams together.

Unroll the jelly roll, and spread with 3 tablespoons cream, then the chestnut purée mixture. Sprinkle with half the grated chocolate or chocolate curls, reserving the best ones for decoration. Re-roll the jelly roll and place on a serving dish. Spread the remaining cream over the top and sides and decorate with the reserved grated chocolate or chocolate curls.

BLACK FOREST GÂTEAU

5 eggs
1¼ cups caster sugar
1 cup self-rising flour
¼ cup cocoa powder
4 tablespoons vegetable oil

FILLING AND DECORATION
1 lb frozen pitted black cherries, thawed
1 tablespoon arrowroot
6 tablespoons Kirsch
1½ cups heavy cream
1½ cups confectioners sugar, sifted
2 oz chocolate caraque (page 10)

Grease and line a 9 inch round cake pan. Beat the eggs and sugar until thick and creamy, and the beater leaves a trail when lifted out of the mixture. Sift in the flour and cocoa and fold into the mixture. Fold in the oil.

Turn the mixture into the prepared pan and bake in a moderately hot oven, 357°F, for about 30 minutes. Allow to cool in the pan for 5 minutes, then turn out on to a wire rack and leave to cool.

To make the filling and decoration, drain the juice from the cherries. Blend the arrowroot with 3 tablespoons of the cherry syrup. Heat the remainder of the syrup to just below boiling point, then pour over the blended arrowroot. Return to the pan and bring back to the boil, stirring all the time, until thickened. Remove from the heat and stir in the pitted cherries, then stir in 3 tablespoons of the Kirsch. Leave to cool. Whip the cream until it holds its shape, then fold in the remaining Kirsch and the confectioners sugar.

Split the cake into three rounds. Place the bottom round on a serving plate, spread with some of the cream and half the cherries, place the second round on top, spread with more cream and the rest of the cherries, and then top with the last round. Spread the remaining cream over the cake, bringing it up into swirls. Decorate the top with the chocolate caraque and chill until ready to serve.

RASPBERRY LAYER CAKE

4 eggs, separated
grated rind and juice of 1 lemon
1¼ cups confectioners sugar, sifted
¾ cup flour
3 tablespoons cornstarch
½ teaspoon baking soda

FILLING
14 oz canned raspberries
2 teaspoons powdered gelatin
3 cups heavy cream
2 tablespoons caster sugar
3 oz bitter chocolate, grated

Grease and line an 8 inch round cake pan. Beat together the egg yolks, lemon rind and juice and confectioners sugar until thick and creamy, and the beater leaves a trail when lifted out of the mixture. Beat the egg whites until they form stiff peaks. Sift together the flour, cornstarch and baking soda and gently fold into the egg yolks, one-third at a time, with the egg whites.

Turn the mixture into the prepared pan and bake in a medium oven, 350°F, for 35–40 minutes. Remove from the oven and leave to cool in the pan for 5 minutes. Turn out on to a wire rack and leave to cool. When the cake is quite cold, split into three rounds.

To make the filling, drain the raspberries, reserving the juice. Put 2 tablespoons of juice in a bowl and sprinkle the gelatin on top. Leave to soften for 5 minutes. Stand the bowl over a pan of simmering water and leave until the gelatin has dissolved. Remove from the heat and allow to cool slightly. Whip two-thirds of the cream lightly and then beat in the gelatin and sugar. Add the raspberries to the cream, then add the chocolate and fold in gently. Put the filling to one side and leave until set.

Spread each layer of sponge evenly with the filling, and sandwich together. Whip the remaining cream until stiff and pipe over the top of the cake. Chill for 1 hour before serving.

TIPSY CAKE

¾ cup self-rising flour
¼ cup cocoa powder
4 eggs
½ cup caster sugar
3 tablespoons corn oil

SYRUP
¾ cup granulated sugar
2 tablespoons instant coffee granules
1½ cups water
3 tablespoons brandy **or** dark rum
1 cup whipping cream

DECORATION
coffee beans

Grease and line an 8 inch cake pan. Sift together the flour and cocoa powder. Beat the eggs and sugar until thick and creamy, and the beater leaves a trail when lifted out of the mixture. Fold in the flour and cocoa, then fold in the corn oil very carefully.

Turn the mixture into the prepared pan and bake in a medium oven, 350°F, for 45 minutes. Remove from the oven and allow to cool in the pan for 5 minutes, then turn out on to a wire rack and leave to cool.

To make the syrup, put the sugar and coffee in the water in a small pan and stir over low heat until the sugar has dissolved. Bring to the boil. Remove from the heat and add the brandy or the rum.

Place the cake on a serving plate and prick all over with a skewer. Pour over a little of the hot coffee syrup and allow it to soak in. Pour over a little more and continue doing this until all the syrup has been absorbed. Leave to stand for at least 2 hours.

Whip the cream until thick but not stiff and spread it all over the top and sides of the cake. Swirl into a pattern with a fork. Decorate with a few coffee beans.

CARIBBEAN GÂTEAU

4 eggs, separated
¼ cup caster sugar
4 tablespoons very hot water
(see **Note**)
¾ cup flour
¼ cup cocoa powder
1½ teaspoons baking soda

FILLING AND DECORATION
15 oz canned mangoes
1 cup whipping cream
2 chocolate flake bars, crumbled

Grease and line an 8 inch round baking pan. Beat the egg yolks with the sugar until thick and creamy. Gradually beat in the very hot water. Beat until thick and creamy, and the beater leaves a trail when lifted out of the mixture. Sift in the flour, cocoa and baking soda, and fold in. Beat the egg whites until stiff, then fold gently into the mixture.

Turn the mixture into the prepared pan and bake in a medium oven, 350°F, for about 50 minutes, or until the cake springs back when pressed lightly. Allow to cool in the pan for 5 minutes, then turn out on to a wire rack and leave to cool. When cold, split the cake into three rounds.

To make the filling, drain the mangoes, reserving the syrup. Set aside about three of the best mango slices for decoration and chop the remainder. Whip the cream lightly with 2 tablespoons of the mango syrup.

Spread the bottom round of the cake with a third of the cream, half the chopped mango pieces and a third of the chocolate flake. Place the next layer of cake on top, and spread with another third of the cream, the mangoes and chocolate flake. Top with the last round of cake, and spread with the last of the cream. Decorate with the reserved mango slices and the remainder of the chocolate flake.

Note It is particularly important that the water is hot but not actually boiling. A kettle with boiling water left for a few minutes, once boiled, will be the right temperature.

CHOCOLATE PEPPERMINT ROLL

3 eggs
⅓ cup caster sugar
½ cup self-rising flour
2 tablespoons cocoa powder

FILLING AND FROSTING
⅓ cup butter
1 cup confectioners sugar, sifted
a few drops peppermint extract
8 tablespoons evaporated milk
2 teaspoons cocoa powder
4 oz compound chocolate,
broken into small pieces

Grease and line a 13×9 inch jelly roll pan. Beat the eggs and sugar until thick and creamy, and the beater leaves a trail when lifted out of the mixture. Sift in the flour and cocoa, and fold in.

Turn the mixture into the prepared pan and spread evenly. Bake in a moderately hot oven, 400°F, for about 12 minutes or until the cake springs back when pressed lightly. Turn on to a piece of wax or non-stick silicon paper, dredged with confectioners or powdered sugar. Carefully peel off the lining paper, trim off the edges and quickly roll up the jelly roll, keeping the paper inside. Allow to cool.

To make the filling, cream the butter, beat in the confectioners sugar, then beat in the peppermint extract. Unroll the jelly roll, spread with the butter frosting and re-roll. Place on a wire rack with a plate underneath.

Put the evaporated milk and cocoa into a small pan and bring to the boil. Remove from the heat and stir in the chocolate. Stir until the chocolate has melted, returning to gentle heat, if necessary. Put to one side and allow to cool, beating from time to time until the frosting is quite thick and glossy; do not worry if it becomes too thick and set as this is easier to use than a runny frosting. Pour the chocolate frosting evenly over the cake and leave to set.

Caribbean Gâteau

BÛCHE DE NOEL

4 eggs
½ cup caster sugar
¾ cup self-rising flour
¼ cup cocoa powder

FILLING AND FROSTING
½ cup milk
2 egg yolks
6 oz semisweet chocolate, broken into small pieces
½ cup unsalted butter
½ cup confectioners sugar, sifted
extra confectioners sugar
holly **or** other Christmas cake decorations

Grease and line a 13×9 inch jelly roll pan. Beat the eggs and sugar together until thick and creamy, and the beater leaves a trail when lifted out of the mixture. Sift in the flour and cocoa, and fold in. Turn the mixture into the prepared pan.

Bake in a moderately hot oven, 400°F, for 12–15 minutes or until the cake springs back when pressed lightly. Turn out on to a piece of wax or non-stick silicon paper dredged with confectioners or caster sugar. Carefully peel off the lining paper, trim off the edges, and roll up the jelly roll, keeping the paper inside the roll. Allow to cool.

To make the filling, heat the milk to blood temperature in a small saucepan. Blend the egg yolks in a bowl or the top of a double boiler, and beat in the milk. Stand the mixture over a pan of gently simmering water, and cook, stirring frequently, until the mixture coats the back of a wooden spoon. Add the chocolate, and stir until it has melted, then remove from the heat. Cover the bowl with a piece of clingfilm and leave to cool, stirring from time to time. Cream the butter and beat in the confectioners sugar, then gradually beat in the cooled custard.

Unroll the jelly roll, and spread with a third of the filling. Re-roll and spread the outside of the roll with the remaining frosting.

Using a fork, mark lines on the top of the log, as if for the bark of a tree. Chill for about 1 hour until set, then sprinkle all over with confectioners sugar, and decorate with holly, cake decorations, etc.

PEAR AND CHOCOLATE GÂTEAU

¾ cup self-rising flour
¼ cup cocoa powder
4 eggs
½ cup caster sugar

FILLING AND TOPPING
4 oz semisweet chocolate, broken into pieces
2 egg yolks
¼ cup whipping cream
2 ripe pears
1 tablespoon lemon juice

Make the filling first. Melt the chocolate (page 11). Remove from the heat and beat in the egg yolks, one at a time. Beat in 1 tablespoon of the cream. Whip the remainder of the cream, then fold into the chocolate mixture. Chill for 1 hour.

Grease and line two 8½–9 inch layer-cake pans. Sift together the flour and cocoa. Beat the eggs and sugar until thick and creamy, and the beater leaves a trail when lifted out of the mixture. Fold in the flour.

Turn the mixture into the prepared tins. Bake in a moderately hot oven, 375°F, for 15–20 minutes, or until well risen and the cakes spring back when pressed lightly. Allow to cool in the pans for 5 minutes, then turn out on to a wire rack and leave to cool.

Peel the pears and slice them thinly. Dip in the lemon juice to preserve the color. When the cakes are quite cold, spread one of them with half the chocolate filling. Cover with two-thirds of the pears, and place the second cake on top. Spread with the last of the chocolate mixture and arrange the remaining pears on top.

DOBOS TORTE

4 eggs, separated
1½ cups caster sugar
1 cup ground hazelnuts (see **Note**)

FILLING
4 oz semisweet chocolate, broken into pieces
½ cup unsalted butter
½ cup confectioners sugar, sifted

TOPPING
¾ cup granulated sugar
3 tablespoons water
a few whole hazelnuts

Grease and line two 7 inch layer-cake pans, preferably with non-stick silicon paper. Beat the egg yolks and sugar until thick and creamy. Beat the egg whites until they form stiff peaks. Fold the hazelnuts and egg whites alternately into the egg yolks.

Divide the mixture between the two pans and bake in a medium oven, 350°F, for 30 minutes or until set. Allow to cool in the pans for 10 minutes, then turn out on to a wire rack and leave to cool.

To make the filling, melt the chocolate (page 11). Cream the butter and confectioners sugar, then beat in the chocolate. Use half of the mixture to sandwich together the two cakes.

To make the topping, put the sugar and water into a small pan and stir over low heat until the sugar has dissolved. Bring to the boil and boil rapidly to 345°F on a candy thermometer (caramel stage). Using an oiled knife, spread the caramel evenly over the top of the cake. While it is still soft, mark into eight portions with a sharp knife and leave to set.

Put the remaining buttercream into a pastry bag and pipe round the edge of the cake. Decorate with a few whole hazelnuts.

Note Whole hazelnuts, ground in a blender or food processor can also be used.

REFRIGERATOR COOKIE CAKE

4 oz semisweet chocolate, broken into small pieces
¼ cup unsalted butter
3 egg yolks
⅓ cup caster sugar
6 tablespoons water
1 tablespoon granulated sugar
½ cup warm strong black coffee
2 tablespoons dark rum
32 Oreo cookies

DECORATION
chocolate vermicelli

Melt the chocolate (page 11). Remove from the heat and allow to cool slightly. Cream the butter until light and fluffy, then beat in the chocolate.

In a separate bowl, beat the egg yolks lightly. Put the caster sugar and water into a small, heavy-based pan and stir over low heat until the sugar has dissolved. Boil rapidly to 225°F on a candy thermometer (thread stage). Beat into the egg yolks gradually until the mixture has a mousse-like consistency. Add to the butter mixture, a little at a time, and beat well.

Dissolve the granulated sugar in the coffee and add the rum. Quickly dip eight cookies into the coffee syrup and place flat on a plate in two rows. Spread with a little of the chocolate buttercream. Repeat these layers twice more, then finish with a layer of cookies. Spread the remaining chocolate buttercream over the top and sides, and sprinkle with chocolate vermicelli. Chill in a refrigerator for 2 hours or until quite firm.

CHOCOLATE FROSTED GUGELHUPF

1 tablespoon dried yeast
½ cup caster sugar
6 tablespoons warm water
4 cups flour
1 teaspoon salt
¾ cup warm milk
4 eggs, lightly beaten
½ cup butter, well softened
¾ cup raisins
¼ cup chocolate bits
⅓ cup chopped mixed candied peel
¼ cup blanched almonds, chopped coarsely
2 teaspoons vanilla extract
6oz semisweet chocolate, broken into pieces
3 tablespoons water
2 tablespoons dark rum
1½ cups confectioners sugar, sifted

Well butter a 5 pint gugelhupf mold. Dissolve the yeast and 1 teaspoon sugar in the warm water. Sift in ½ cup flour and mix lightly. Leave in a warm place for 30 minutes until risen. Sift the remaining flour with the salt into a mixing bowl. Make a hollow in the center, pour in the yeast liquid, milk and eggs, and beat well. Beat in the butter thoroughly, then beat in the raisins, chocolate bits, peel, almonds and vanilla extract; beat until the mixture is smooth and elastic. Cover with a piece of oiled clingfilm and leave in a warm place for 1 hour or until the mixture has doubled in size.

Turn the dough into the prepared mold, cover again with oiled clingfilm and leave in a warm place for 30 minutes or until it reaches the top of the pan. Bake in a medium oven, 350°F, for 1 hour. Remove from the oven, cool in the pan for 5 minutes, then invert on to a cooling rack and leave to cool.

To make the frosting, melt the chocolate with the water and rum (page 11). Keeping the pan over the heat, gradually beat in the confectioners sugar until the frosting is smooth and shiny. Remove from the heat and allow to cool and thicken slightly, then pour evenly over the gugelhupf and leave to set.

LOGANBERRY CAKE

4 eggs, separated
½ cup caster sugar
¼ cup cocoa powder
1 cup fresh white breadcrumbs
1 cup ground almonds

FILLING AND TOPPING
½ cup heavy cream
4 tablespoons loganberry jam **or** conserve

DECORATION (optional)
a few fresh loganberries **or** raspberries

Grease and line an 8 inch cake pan. Beat the egg yolks and sugar until thick and creamy. Sift in the cocoa powder and fold in with the breadcrumbs. Beat the egg whites until stiff, then fold half into the mixture. Fold in the almonds, then the remainder of the egg whites, taking care to lose as little air as possible.

Turn the mixture into the prepared pan and bake in a medium oven, 350°F, for 45 minutes. Remove from the oven and allow to cool.

When the cake is quite cold, carefully split in half. Whip the cream until stiff, and fill the center of the cake with half the cream and the loganberry jam or conserve. Pipe the remaining cream over the top and decorate with fresh loganberries or raspberries, if liked.

Loganberry Cake

CHOCOLATE GINGER SQUARES

Makes 9

1¼ cups flour
¼ cup cocoa powder
½ teaspoon salt
2 teaspoons baking soda
½ cup light soft brown sugar
2 eggs, separated
6 tablespoons corn oil
6 tablespoons milk
2 tablespoons candied ginger, chopped finely

FROSTING
2 tablespoons butter
¼ cup cocoa powder
3 tablespoons hot water
2 cups confectioners sugar, sifted
2 tablespoons candied ginger, chopped finely

Grease and line a 7 inch square cake pan. Sift together the flour, cocoa, salt and baking soda into a bowl. Add the sugar. Blend the egg yolks, oil and milk. Pour into the center of the dry ingredients and beat well. Mix in the ginger. Beat the egg whites until stiff, then fold gently into the mixture.

Turn the mixture into the prepared pan and bake in a medium oven, 350°F, for about 45 minutes, or until well risen and firm. Remove from the oven, allow to cool in the pan for 5 minutes, then turn out on to a wire rack and leave to cool.

To make the frosting, melt the butter in a pan. Blend the cocoa with the hot, not boiling, water, then pour into the confectioners sugar in a bowl. Add the butter and beat well to give a thick glossy frosting (use a little extra water if necessary). Add the ginger and beat well. Pour evenly over the top of the cake. Leave to set. Cut into squares to serve.

CHERRY FINGERS

Makes 16

¾ cup butter
¼ cup caster sugar
4 eggs, separated
a pinch of salt
1 cup instant chocolate milk mix
½ cup ground almonds
¼ cup flour, sifted

FILLING AND DECORATION
¼ cup butter
¼ cup cream cheese
½ cup confectioners sugar, sifted
4 tablespoons good quality black cherry jam
extra confectioners sugar

Grease and line a 13×9 inch jelly roll pan. Cream the butter and sugar until light and fluffy. Beat in the egg yolks with the salt, one at a time. Sift in the instant chocolate milk mix, and fold in. Fold in the ground almonds and flour. Beat the egg whites until stiff, then fold in gently, a third at a time (the mixture may look curdled at this stage, but this does not matter).

Turn the mixture into the prepared pan and spread evenly. Bake in a medium oven, 350°F, for about 25 minutes. Turn out on to a sheet of wax paper on a wire tray. Peel off the lining paper carefully. Leave to cool, then cut the cake in half to make two squares.

To make the filling, cream the butter with the cream cheese and confectioners sugar. Spread over one of the squares of cake. Spread the cherry jam on top and sandwich the cakes together. Cut in half, then cut each half into eight fingers. Dust with confectioners sugar before serving.

CHOCOLATE ÉCLAIRS

Makes about 12

10 tablespoons flour
a pinch of salt
¼ cup butter, cut into small pieces
½ cup water
2 eggs
1 egg yolk

FILLING AND FROSTING
1 cup heavy cream
1 egg white
1 tablespoon confectioners sugar
6 oz semisweet chocolate, broken into pieces

Sift together the flour and salt on to a sheet of wax paper. Put the butter into a pan with the water. Put over gentle heat until the butter has melted, then bring to the boil. Remove the pan from the heat, add the flour all at once and beat well until the mixture forms a soft ball and leaves the sides of the pan clean. If necessary, replace the pan over very low heat. Allow to cool slightly, then beat in the whole eggs and the egg yolk, one at a time, until a very smooth, shiny mixture results.

Put the pastry into a pastry bag fitted with a ½ inch plain tip and pipe out 3 inch lengths on to greased cookie sheets; allow plenty of room on the trays for the éclairs to rise and spread.

Bake the éclairs in a moderately hot oven, 400°F, for about 25 minutes, or until golden-brown. Remove from the oven, make a couple of slits in the sides of each one to allow the steam to escape and return to the oven for a further 5–10 minutes to dry out. Remove from the oven and leave to cool on a wire rack.

To make the filling, whip the cream until stiff. Beat the egg white until it forms stiff peaks, then beat in the confectioners sugar, 1 teaspoon at a time. Fold into the cream. Make a slit down the side of each éclair and fill with the cream, or pipe it in.

Melt the chocolate (page 11), then pour into a container long enough to be able to dip the top surface of each éclair into the chocolate. Dip the tops of the éclairs into the chocolate, then leave to set.

MIXED NUT SLICE

Makes 15

⅓ cup butter
2 tablespoons caster sugar
1 egg yolk
½ teaspoon vanilla extract
1 cup flour
1 tablespoon cocoa powder

FILLING
2 eggs
½ cup soft brown sugar
¼ cup chopped mixed nuts
¾ cup shredded coconut

TOPPING
2 tablespoons chopped mixed nuts
2 tablespoons shredded coconut
¾ cup semisweet **or** milk chocolate bits,
broken into pieces

Butter a 7×11 inch jelly roll pan. Cream the butter and sugar until light and fluffy, then beat in the egg yolk and vanilla extract. Sift in the flour and cocoa and form into a stiff dough. Turn on to a lightly floured surface and knead lightly. Roll out to a rectangle a little smaller than the pan, then lift into the pan and press into the edges.

To make the filling, beat the eggs and sugar until thick and creamy, and the beater leaves a trail when lifted out of the mixture. Fold in the nuts and coconut, then spread evenly over the chocolate base. Sprinkle with the nuts and coconut for the topping.

Bake in a moderately hot oven, 375°F, for 20–25 minutes or until golden-brown. Remove from the oven and allow to cool in the pan. When cold, cut into 15 squares.

Melt the chocolate bits and drizzle over the nut slices (page 10). Leave to set.

CHOCOLATE CROISSANTS

Makes 8

1 teaspoon sugar
⅓ cup plus 1 tablespoon warm water
2 teaspoons dried yeast
2 cups bread flour
1 teaspoon salt
2 tablespoons shortening
¼ cup caster sugar
1 egg, lightly beaten
⅓ cup butter
½ cup milk chocolate bits

EGG GLAZE
1 egg
1 tablespoon water
½ teaspoon caster sugar

Dissolve the sugar in the water in a bowl, sprinkle with the yeast and leave in a warm place for 10 minutes or until frothy. Sift together the flour and salt, rub in the shortening and mix in the sugar. Make a well in the center of the flour, pour in the yeast liquid and the egg, and mix to a soft dough. Turn on to a lightly floured surface and knead well for about 5 minutes. When the dough feels smooth and elastic, roll it out to a rectangle about 12 × 5 inches.

Divide the butter into three. Dot the top two-thirds of the dough with one part of the butter, cut into small pieces. Fold the bottom third up and the top third down, like an envelope. Seal the edges, give the dough a half turn, then roll out again and repeat this process with the remaining two parts of butter. Fold the dough, put into an oiled polythene bag and chill for at least 1 hour.

Roll out to a 12 inch square, cover with a piece of oiled clingfilm and leave for 10–15 minutes. Trim the edges, divide into four squares, then divide each of these into two triangles.

To make the egg glaze, beat the egg with the water and sugar. Brush all over the dough, then sprinkle with the chocolate bits. Roll each triangle up loosely, starting from the wide side and going towards the point.

Place the croissants on oiled cookie sheets, with the tip underneath, and curve into crescents. Brush again with the egg glaze and cover with oiled clingfilm. Put in a warm place and leave until the dough has doubled in size, then remove the clingfilm, brush again with the egg glaze and bake in a hot oven, 425°F, for 15–20 minutes or until well risen and golden-brown. Remove from the oven and cool on a wire rack.

CHOCOLATE AND ALMOND SLICES

Makes 18

1¾ cups flour
1 teaspoon baking soda
¼ cup cocoa powder
½ cup butter
½ cup soft brown sugar
2 tablespoons corn syrup
a little milk
¼ cup flaked almonds

Well butter a 11 × 7 inch jelly roll pan. Sift together the flour, baking soda and cocoa. Cream the butter and sugar until light and fluffy, then beat in the syrup. Gradually work in the dry ingredients to make a smooth dough.

Press into the prepared pan and prick all over with a fork. Brush with a little milk and sprinkle with the almonds. Bake in a medium oven, 350°F, for about 30 minutes or until golden-brown, then cool in the pan and mark into fingers while still warm.

BROWNIES
Makes 16

2 oz semisweet chocolate
½ cup butter
¾ cup soft brown sugar
¾ cup self-rising flour, sifted
2 eggs, beaten
½ cup walnuts, chopped roughly

Grease and flour a shallow 8 inch square cake pan. Melt the chocolate and butter (page 11). Remove from the heat and stir in the sugar. Beat in the flour and eggs until smooth. Stir in the walnuts.

Pour the mixture into the prepared pan and bake in a medium oven, 350°F, for 35–40 minutes until well risen and firm to the touch; the inside should be slightly soft and the surface cracked. Cool slightly before cutting into squares or bars.

FLORENTINES
Makes about 8

¼ cup butter
¼ cup caster sugar
¼ cup flour, sifted
½ cup blanched almonds, chopped
¼ cup candied cherries, chopped
¼ cup candied peel, chopped
4 oz semisweet chocolate, broken into pieces

Line two cookie sheets with non-stick silicon paper. Put the butter and sugar into a small pan and heat gently until melted. Remove from the heat and stir in the flour with the almonds, cherries and peel.

Drop spoonfuls of the mixture, well apart, on to the prepared cookie sheets. Bake in a medium oven, 350°F, for about 10 minutes until golden-brown. Leave to cool on the cookie sheets until set, then lift on to a cooling rack.

Melt the chocolate (page 11). Spread over the smooth sides of the cookies. Before it sets, mark in wavy lines with the prongs of a fork.

COCONUT MERINGUE SLICES
Makes 14

½ cup butter **or** margarine
2 cups flour, sifted
cold water
1¾ cups semisweet chocolate chips
2 egg whites
½ cup caster sugar
1 cup shredded coconut

Rub the fat into the flour until the mixture resembles fine breadcrumbs. Bind with cold water to form a firm dough. Roll out on a floured surface and use to line the base and sides of a 7×11 inch jelly roll pan. Sprinkle the chocolate over the pastry. Beat the egg whites until they form stiff peaks, then beat in half the sugar, 1 teaspoon at a time until the mixture is stiff and shiny. Fold in the remaining sugar and the coconut. Spoon it over the chocolate and spread evenly, using a spatula, until the chocolate is completely covered.

Bake in a medium oven, 350°F, for 30 minutes. Remove from the oven and allow to cool slightly. Cut into slices while still warm.

CHOCOLATE MERINGUES

Makes 6

3 egg whites
⅓ cup caster sugar
¾ cup confectioners sugar
¼ cup cocoa powder
¼ cup whipping cream (optional)

Lightly oil a cookie sheet and line with non-stick silicon paper. Beat the egg whites until they form stiff peaks. Gradually beat in the caster sugar, 1 teaspoon at a time until the mixture is stiff and shiny. Sift together the confectioners sugar and cocoa and fold into the mixture.

Either put the mixture in a pastry bag fitted with a large rose tip, and pipe 12 meringues on to the prepared cookie sheet, or put 12 heaped spoonfuls of the mixture on to the cookie sheet. Bake in a very cool oven, 250°F, for 1 hour. Reduce the heat as much as possible and cook for a further 4 hours, or until the meringues are quite dry. Remove from the oven and allow to cool. For serving, whip the cream lightly, if used, and sandwich the meringues together, two at a time, with the cream.

CRUNCHY DATE BARS

Makes 10

½ lb Graham crackers
½ cup butter
3 tablespoons Demerara sugar
2 cups dried dates, chopped
¼ cup raisins
4 oz semisweet chocolate **or** compound chocolate, broken into pieces

Lightly butter a 9 inch layer-cake pan. Put the Graham crackers in a polythene bag and crush with a rolling-pin, or use a food processor. Heat the butter and sugar gently in a pan until the butter has melted and the sugar dissolved. Remove from the heat and add the dates and raisins. Stir in the cracker crumbs and blend well.

Spread the mixture evenly over the base of the prepared pan and press down firmly. Melt the chocolate (page 11) and spread over the cookie mixture. Mark out bars with a sharp knife while the chocolate is still slightly soft. Leave to set for at least 1 hour. Cut into bars to serve.

CHOCOLATE CHIP COOKIES

Makes about 36

$\frac{1}{4}$ cup butter
$\frac{1}{2}$ cup caster sugar
1 egg, beaten
$\frac{1}{2}$ teaspoon vanilla extract
$1\frac{1}{4}$ cups wholewheat flour
a pinch of salt
3 tablespoons milk
1 cup semisweet chocolate bits

Well grease three or four large cookie sheets. Cream the butter and sugar until light and fluffy. Beat in the egg and vanilla extract gradually. Sift in the flour and salt, and fold in with the milk and chocolate bits.

Put spoonfuls of the mixture on to the prepared cookie sheets, spacing them well apart. Bake in a medium oven, 350°F, for about 12–15 minutes or until golden-brown. Leave to cool on the cookie sheets for 1 minute, then remove with a spatula and cool on a wire rack.

CHOCOLATE FLAPJACKS

Makes 12

$\frac{1}{3}$ cup butter
$\frac{1}{3}$ cup light soft brown sugar
2 tablespoons corn syrup
1 cup rolled oats
4 oz bitter chocolate, broken into pieces

Grease a shallow 7 inch square pan. Put the butter, sugar and syrup in a pan over low heat, and stir until the fat has melted and the sugar has dissolved. Remove from the heat and stir in the rolled oats.

Press the mixture into the prepared pan, spreading evenly. Bake in a medium oven, 350°F, for about 20 minutes until golden-brown. Remove from the oven. While still warm, mark out into fingers with a sharp knife. Leave in the pan to cool.

Melt the chocolate (page 11), and pour over the cooled flapjacks, spreading to the edges in an even frosting. Leave to set, then remove from the pan and cut into fingers.

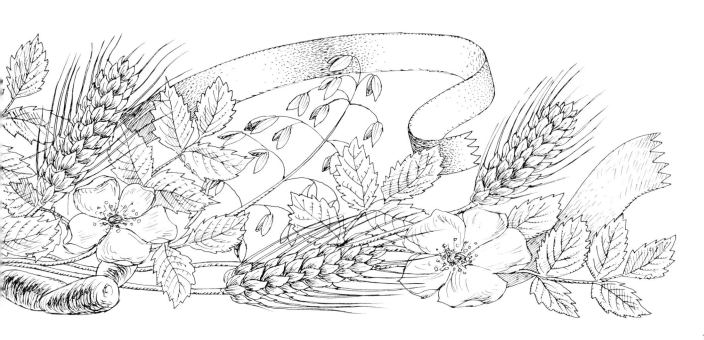

CHOCOLATE COOKIE SQUARES

Makes 25

6 oz oreo cookies
½ cup butter
⅓ cup corn syrup
¼ cup cocoa powder
½ cup seedless raisins
½ cup candied cherries, chopped finely
¼ cup blanched almonds, chopped
25 chocolate chips

Grease a shallow 7 inch square cake pan. Put the cookies in a polythene bag and crush with a rolling-pin, or use a food processor. Heat the butter, syrup and cocoa gently until the fat has melted. Remove from the heat and stir in first the raisins, cherries and almonds and then the cookie crumbs. Stir until thoroughly mixed.

Press the mixture into the prepared pan and space the chocolate chips evenly on top in lines of five. Leave in a cool place to set, then cut into squares, between the chips.

CHOCOLATE CHIP SHORTCAKE

Makes 10

1 cup flour
½ cup cornstarch
¼ cup caster sugar
½ cup butter
¼ cup milk chocolate bits

Sift together the flour and cornstarch. Add the sugar, then rub in the butter. The mixture will become crumbly at first, but continue working it until it clings together in heavy lumps. Turn on to a board or working surface dusted with flour or cornstarch and knead lightly. Place the ball on a buttered cookie sheet and roll out to make a 9 inch circle. Prick the surface with a fork. Mark out 10 portions with a sharp knife and flute the edges with your fingers. Sprinkle with the chocolate bits.

Bake in a warm oven, 325°F, for 30–35 minutes or until the shortcake is cooked; but it should not be browned. Remove from the oven and leave to cool on the cookie sheet for 10 minutes, then, using a spatula, lift carefully on to a wire rack to cool.

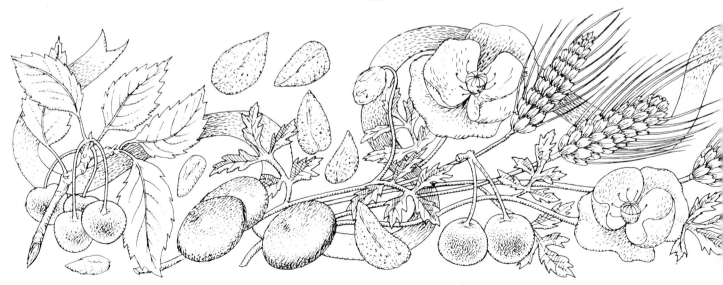

PINEAPPLE SHORTCAKES

Makes 8

1¼ cups flour
¼ cup instant cocoa powder
a pinch of salt
½ cup butter
½ cup heavy cream
2 cups canned pineapple rings, drained

Sift together the flour, instant cocoa powder and salt. Rub in the butter until the mixture is crumbly, then knead together until smooth. Roll out on a floured surface and cut into eight 4 inch diameter circles.

Put the shortcakes on to greased cookie sheets and bake in a warm oven, 325°F, for about 15 minutes. Remove from the oven and allow to cool on the sheet for 5 minutes. Transfer to a wire rack and leave to cool. Whip the cream until stiff, and divide between the cookies. Cut the pineapple rings into quarters and place two pieces on each cookie.

SHORTCAKE ZIG-ZAGS

Makes 12

1¼ cups flour
¼ cup caster sugar
½ cup butter
2 tablespoons instant cocoa powder

Well butter a 7 inch square cake pan. Sift all but 2 tablespoons of the flour into a bowl. Add the sugar, then rub in the butter until the mixture is crumbly. Divide the mixture in half. Work in the remaining flour to one half and the instant cocoa powder to the other. Turn on to a board or working surface lightly dusted with flour, and knead each dough separately until smooth. Roll out and cut into strips 1½ inches wide. Put these strips diagonally across the pan; any trimmings can be cut into shapes and baked on a cookie sheet.

Bake in a warm oven, 325°F, for about 30–35 minutes, or until crisp but not brown (trimmings will only take about 5 minutes). Remove from the oven, mark out into fingers and leave to cool in the pan.

CHOCOLATE SANDWICH COOKIES

Makes about 20

½ cup butter
½ cup caster sugar
2 tablespoons beaten egg
½ teaspoon vanilla extract
2 cups flour, sifted

FILLING
⅓ cup butter
¾ cup soft brown sugar
¼ cup semisweet chocolate bits

Cream together the butter and sugar until pale and creamy. Beat in the egg and vanilla extract, a little at a time, alternating with some of the flour. Stir in the remaining flour to give a firm dough. Knead the dough until smooth, then roll out on a floured surface to a thickness of about ¼ inch. Stamp out circles with a 2 inch fluted cookie cutter.

Place the circles on greased cookie sheets and prick with a fork. Re-roll the trimmings and cut out more cookies. Bake in a medium oven, 350°F, for about 15 minutes until golden. Leave on the sheets to harden for a few minutes, then remove to a wire rack and allow to cool.

To make the filling, beat together the butter and sugar until pale and creamy. Melt the chocolate (page 11). Beat into the creamed mixture, then leave to thicken slightly. Sandwich the cookies together, two at a time, with some of the chocolate frosting.

TUILES

Makes about 30

2 egg whites
1 cup caster sugar
½ cup flour, sifted
⅔ cup flaked almonds
¼ cup butter, melted
a few drops almond extract
4 oz semisweet chocolate, broken into small pieces

Lightly beat the egg whites in a mixing bowl until they are frothy. Beat in the sugar and continue beating until the sugar is well mixed in. Fold in the flour, flaked almonds, butter and almond extract.

Put teaspoonfuls of the mixture on to greased cookie sheets, spacing them well apart to allow for spreading; you will probably have to do this in batches. Bake in a moderately hot oven, 375°F, for about 6 minutes, or until golden-brown. Carefully lift the cookies off the sheet with a spatula, and place on greased rolling-pins to cool; this gives the cookies their traditional curled shape.

Melt the chocolate (page 11). Take each cooled cookie, one at a time, and dip each end in the chocolate, to a depth of about ½ inch. Lay on a sheet of waxed or non-stick silicon paper and leave until the chocolate has set. Store in an airtight tin.

DESSERTS AND ICES

This is where the chocolate cook comes into his or her own, and can create a plethora of truly delicious concoctions from delicate, light steamed hot desserts and soufflés to creamy ices, and on to mousses, fools and meringue-based desserts. All are wickedly sinful which is perhaps part of their strong attraction.

Chocolate mousse – that delectable dessert – comes in a variety of different shapes and forms. One of the best ways of serving it is in a chocolate case, either small individual ones, like the Chocolate and Crème de Menthe Mousses on page 47, or in a single larger case, like that used for the Strawberry Chocolate Box on page 48.

A very simple, yet impressive looking dessert using the same principle can be made by lining individual patty pans as for the Easter Eggs on page 68, and then filling the completed case with whipped cream and fresh fruit.

There is little to beat home-made ice cream made with fresh cream and eggs. One of my great favorites is the Chocolate Terrine with Cherry Sauce on page 63 – a wonderfully rich chocolate ice, which will keep for months in a freezer, so that you need never find yourself without a really good dessert at the last minute.

As chocolate teams well with just about every fruit and seems to have a natural affinity for nuts, there is no end to the variations one can try within the recipes. For example, peaches, strawberries or raspberries could be used instead of the apricots in the Apricot Fruit Basket on page 51, whilst other sorbet flavors can be used for the Lemon Sorbet with Raspberry Sauce on page 66. The idea of coating balls of sorbet with chocolate can also be extended to ice cream and I have served small balls of ice cream, coated in chocolate, with a hot cherry sauce. So let your imagination have full rein and use the recipes in this chapter to help you create some of your own 'personalized' recipes.

HOT CHOCOLATE SOUFFLÉ

Serves 4

4oz semisweet chocolate, broken into pieces
2 tablespoons water **or** liqueur
½ cup caster sugar
4 eggs, separated
confectioners sugar

Butter a 1 quart soufflé dish. Melt the chocolate with the water or liqueur (page 11). Beat together the sugar and yolks until thick and pale. Beat in the melted chocolate until well blended. Beat the egg whites until stiff, then fold in gently.

Pour the mixture into the prepared soufflé dish and bake in a moderately hot oven, 375°F, for about 30 minutes until well risen and firm, but slightly wobbly. Dust the top with confectioners sugar and serve at once.

ORANGE COCOA SOUFFLÉ

Serves 4

2 tablespoons butter **or** margarine
¼ cup flour, sifted
½ cup milk
¼ cup cocoa powder
⅓ cup caster sugar
grated rind and juice of 1 orange
4 eggs, separated
confectioners sugar

Butter a 1½ quart soufflé dish. Melt the fat in a pan and stir in the flour. Add the milk and bring to the boil, stirring until thick and smooth. Add the cocoa, sugar and grated orange rind and juice. Return to the boil, stirring until well blended, then remove from the heat and leave to cool. Add the egg yolks, one at a time, beating until smooth. Beat the egg whites until stiff, then fold gently into the chocolate sauce.

Pour the mixture into the prepared soufflé dish. Bake in a moderate oven, 350°F, for about 45 minutes until well risen and firm, but slightly wobbly. Dust the top with confectioners sugar and serve at once.

Steamed Chocolate Pudding with Orange Sauce

Serves 6

1 medium-sized orange
¼ cup butter
¼ cup caster sugar
3 eggs, beaten
1¼ cups self-rising flour
¼ cup cocoa powder

SAUCE
2 tablespoons butter, preferably unsalted
grated rind and juice of 1 orange
2 teaspoons flour
¼ cup caster sugar
1 egg, separated

DECORATION (optional)
orange rind, pared

Well butter a 1 quart pudding bowl. Thinly pare the orange rind, then cut into matchstick pieces. Cream together the butter, sugar and orange shreds until the mixture is light and fluffy. Beat in the eggs, a little at a time, adding 1 tablespoon of flour with the last amount of egg. Sift in the remaining flour and the cocoa and fold this into the mixture.

Turn the mixture into the prepared bowl, cover with a double piece of buttered wax paper or with foil, and steam for 1¾–2 hours (add more water to the pan if necessary). Turn out of the bowl, decorate with the orange rind, if used, and serve with the orange sauce.

To make the sauce, cream the butter with the orange rind and gradually beat in the flour mixed with the sugar, then add the egg yolk. Make the orange juice up to ½ cup with water, and beat into the mixture; it does not matter if the mixture looks curdled at this stage. Turn the mixture into a small, heavy-based pan and cook over low heat, stirring all the time, until the sauce thickens. Cover the pan with foil and put to one side until ready to serve, then re-heat gently. Beat the egg white until stiff and fold gently into the sauce just before serving.

Variation
Add 2 tablespoons Cointreau or Grand Marnier to the sauce in place of 2 tablespoons water.

Chocolate Soufflé Tart

Serves 6

1½ cups flour
a pinch of salt
⅓ cup butter
cold water

FILLING
2 eggs, separated
2 tablespoons caster sugar
1 tablespoon cornstarch
1 cup light cream
4 oz semisweet chocolate, grated coarsely

Sift together the flour and salt, and rub in the butter until the mixture resembles fine breadcrumbs. Bind together with cold water to make a firm dough. Turn on to a floured surface and knead lightly until smooth. Roll out and use to line an 8 inch flan pan. Prebake in a medium hot oven, 375°F, for 20 minutes.

To make the filling, mix together the egg yolks, sugar and cornstarch. Beat in the cream, then stir in the chocolate, and blend well. Beat the egg whites until they form stiff peaks. Fold gently into the mixture, then turn into the baked pastry case. Bake at 375°F for 25–35 minutes or until the mixture is well risen and golden-brown.

Serve with cream.

Steamed Chocolate Pudding with Orange Sauce

PINEAPPLE AND CHOCOLATE PUDDING

Serves 6

4 slices canned pineapple slices, drained
4 candied cherries
4 oz compound chocolate, broken into pieces
1 teaspoon instant coffee granules
1 teaspoon water
½ cup butter
½ cup caster sugar
2 eggs, separated
¾ cup self-rising flour, sifted

Well butter a 1½ pint pudding bowl. Place one pineapple slice in the base and the remaining three round the sides. Place a cherry in the center of each.

Melt the chocolate with the coffee granules and water (page 11) and remove from the heat. Cream the butter and sugar until light and fluffy, then beat in the egg yolks, one at a time. Beat in the cooled chocolate. Fold the flour into the mixture. Beat the egg whites until they form stiff peaks and fold in.

Turn the mixture into the prepared bowl, cover with a double layer of buttered wax paper or with foil, and steam for 1½ hours (add more water to the pan if necessary). Turn out and serve with a rich chocolate sauce (pages 75–6).

NÉGRE EN CHEMISE

Serves 6

¼ lb sliced white bread, crusts removed
½ cup heavy cream
2 oz semisweet chocolate, broken into pieces
½ cup butter
½ cup ground almonds
¾ cup caster sugar
4 eggs, each beaten separately
½ cup whipping cream
2 tablespoons confectioners sugar, sifted

Well butter a 1 quart mold or dessert bowl. Put the bread into a shallow bowl and pour over the cream. Leave for about 10 minutes, then mash with a fork. Melt the chocolate (page 11). Cream the butter, then, either by hand or, preferably, using an electric beater, beat in the bread, almonds, sugar and chocolate, and continue beating until the mixture is smooth. Beat in the eggs, one at a time.

Turn the mixture into the prepared mold or bowl. Cover with a double layer of buttered wax paper or with foil, and steam for 1½–2 hours (add more boiling water to the pan if necessary).

Whip the cream until stiff and sweeten with the confectioners sugar. Turn the pudding out of the mold or bowl and serve immediately with the cream.

SUSSEX PUDDING

Serves 4–6

2 cups self-rising flour
½ teaspoon salt
¾ cup shredded suet
½ cup water (approx)
½ cup butter, preferably unsalted
2 tablespoons soft brown sugar
¼ cup instant cocoa powder

Well butter a 1 quart pudding bowl. Sift together the flour and salt. Add the suet, then bind with the water to make a soft, but not sticky, dough. Roll out to an 8 inch circle and use to line the prepared bowl.

Cream the butter, then beat in the sugar and instant cocoa powder. Form into a ball and put in the middle of the bowl. Dampen the edges of the pastry, then fold over and press together so that the chocolate ball is completely enclosed. Cover with a double layer of buttered greaseproof paper or with foil, and steam for 2½–3 hours (add more water to the pan if necessary). Turn out and serve with cream.

BAKED PEARS

Serves 4–6

½ cup water
¼ cup sugar
1 vanilla pod
6 large pears, peeled, cored and quartered
4 oz semisweet chocolate, broken into pieces
2 tablespoons butter

Put the water, sugar and vanilla pod into a pan over low heat and stir until the sugar has dissolved. Bring to the boil. Add the pears and poach gently for 10 minutes.

Melt the chocolate with the butter (page 11). Stir in 2 tablespoons of the juice from the pan. Drain the pears, discarding the vanilla pod, and place in a buttered ovenproof pan. Pour over the melted chocolate, cover and bake in a medium oven, 350°F, for 15 minutes.

Serve with ice cream or cream.

SAUCY SPONGE PUDDING

Serves 4–6

¾ cup self-rising flour
¼ cup cocoa powder
a pinch of salt
1 teaspoon baking soda
½ cup soft margarine
½ cup soft brown sugar
2 eggs
½ teaspoon vanilla extract
1 tablespoon milk

SAUCE
½ cup soft brown sugar
¼ cup cocoa powder
1 cup hot water

Well butter a 1 quart baking pan. Sift together the flour, cocoa, salt and baking soda into a mixing bowl. Add the margarine and sugar. Beat the eggs with the vanilla extract and milk, add to the remaining ingredients and beat well for 2 minutes until thoroughly mixed. Spoon into the prepared dish.

To make the sauce, blend together the sugar and cocoa, then gradually stir in the water, and mix well. Pour over the sponge mixture. Bake in a moderately hot oven, 375°F, for 30–40 minutes.

Serve with cream.

Note During cooking, the cake mixture rises above the cocoa/water and sugar mixture to give a light sponge on top with a rich chocolate sauce underneath.

CHOCOLATE EVE'S PUDDING

Serves 4–6

12 oz fresh **or** frozen blackcurrants, thawed
⅓ cup Demerara sugar
½ cup butter **or** margarine
½ cup caster sugar
2 eggs, beaten
¾ cup self-rising flour
¼ cup cocoa powder

Butter a baking pan approximately 7–8 inches in diameter. Put in the blackcurrants and sprinkle with the sugar. Cream the fat and the sugar until light and fluffy. Beat in the eggs, a little at a time, adding 1 tablespoon of the flour with the last amount of egg. Sift in the flour and cocoa and fold into the mixture.

Spoon the mixture over the blackcurrants and spread evenly. Bake in a medium oven, 350°F, for about 40 minutes.

Serve with cream.

RICH CHOCOLATE FONDUE

Serves 6

8 oz semisweet chocolate, broken into pieces
½ cup heavy cream
1½ tablespoons rum, brandy **or** liqueur,
eg Tia Maria, Grand Marnier **or** Cointreau
3 tablespoons blanched almonds, finely chopped

FOR DIPPING
2 lb prepared fresh fruit
(eg pineapple cubes, whole fresh strawberries,
sliced apples, peaches or pears, orange sections, etc)

Place the chocolate in a fondue pot with the cream, and heat very gently, stirring until the chocolate has melted. Stir in the rum, brandy or liqueur and the nuts, then stand over a very gentle flame on a fondue stand.

Use fondue forks to skewer the fruit to dip into the fondue, and serve with crisp cookies or wafers and whipped cream.

ALMOND MOUSSE

Serves 6–8

6 oz semisweet **or** compound chocolate,
broken into pieces
½ cup butter, preferably unsalted
½ cup caster sugar
2 eggs, separated
1½ cups ground almonds
½ cup heavy cream

DECORATION
½ cup blanched whole almonds
½ cup heavy cream

Thoroughly clean and polish a 1 pint jelly mold. Melt the chocolate (page 11), and use to coat the inside of the mold, as when making Easter eggs (page 68); you may find it easier to do this in two layers. When the chocolate is hard, remove from the mold, (do not worry if it cracks very slightly as you can hide this with piping when decorating).

Cream together the butter and sugar until light and fluffy, then beat in the egg yolks, one at a time. Fold in the ground almonds. Whip the cream lightly until it holds its shape. Beat the egg whites until stiff. Fold, first, the cream and then the egg whites into the mixture. Turn into the chocolate mold and chill in a refrigerator for at least 2 hours.

Invert the mold on to a serving plate. Put the almonds on a piece of foil and toast under the broiler until *very lightly* burnt. Remove and leave to cool. Whip the cream until stiff, and pipe on the top and round the edges of the chocolate mold. Decorate with the burnt almonds.

The Chocolate Mousse
Chocolate and Raspberry Layer Mousse (page 46). Chocolate and Crème de Menthe Mousses (page 47), Bitter Chocolate and Orange Mousse (page 46) **and** *Almond Mousse*

CHOCOLATE AND RASPBERRY LAYER MOUSSE

Serves 6–8

RASPBERRY MOUSSE
¼ lb fresh raspberries
1½ teaspoons powdered gelatin
2 tablespoons cold water
2 eggs, separated
¼ cup caster sugar
½ cup heavy **or** whipping cream

CHOCOLATE MOUSSE
6 oz semisweet chocolate, broken into pieces
2 teaspoons instant coffee granules
1 tablespoon water
4 eggs, separated
½ cup heavy **or** whipping cream

DECORATION
¼ cup whipped cream (optional)
a few fresh raspberries

Rub the raspberries through a sieve, or purée in a blender or food processor. Sprinkle the gelatin over the cold water in a bowl and leave to soften for 5 minutes. Stand over a pan of simmering water and leave until the gelatin has dissolved. Remove from the heat and allow to cool slightly. Beat the egg yolks with the sugar until thick and creamy, then beat in the gelatin. Stir in the raspberry purée and blend well. Whip the cream lightly until it holds it shape. Beat the egg whites until stiff. Fold, first, the cream and then the egg whites into the raspberry mixture. Pour into a glass bowl or into individual glasses, and chill in a refrigerator for about 30 minutes.

Melt the chocolate with the coffee granules and water (page 11). Remove from the heat and beat in the egg yolks. Whip the cream lightly until it forms soft peaks. Beat the egg whites until stiff. Fold, first, the cream and then the egg whites into the chocolate mixture. Pour over the raspberry mousse, and chill for at least 1 hour. Decorate with whipped cream, if liked, and raspberries before serving.

BITTER CHOCOLATE AND ORANGE MOUSSE

Serves 6

6 oz bittersweet chocolate, broken into pieces
grated rind and juice of 1 large orange
1 tablespoon cocoa powder
2 tablespoons Grand Marnier
or Cointreau
3 eggs, separated
½ pint heavy cream

DECORATION
whipped cream (optional)
grated orange rind **or** thin matchsticks of orange rind

Melt the chocolate (page 11) with the orange rind and juice and the cocoa. Remove from the heat and beat in the liqueur and egg yolks. Whip the cream until it holds its shape, and beat the egg whites until stiff. Fold, first, the cream and then the egg whites into the chocolate mixture. Turn into six ramekins and chill in a refrigerator for at least 1 hour. Decorate each mousse with a heaped teaspoonful of whipped cream, if liked, and a little orange rind before serving.

Variation
Set the mousse in halved orange shells.

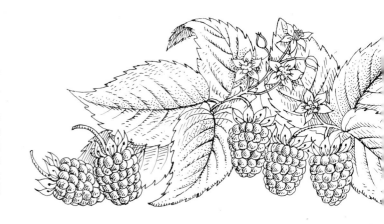

CHOCOLATE AND CRÈME DE MENTHE MOUSSES

Makes 12

10 oz semisweet chocolate, broken into pieces
4 eggs, separated
3 tablespoons crème de menthe

DECORATION
chocolate curls (page 10)

Place 12 paper cake cases in muffin pans. Melt 6 oz of the chocolate (page 11). Divide between the paper cases and, with the back of a teaspoon, spread evenly over the base and sides of the cases. Put in a cool place for at least 30 minutes, or until the chocolate is quite hard.

Peel off the paper cases carefully. Melt the remaining chocolate (page 11) and remove from the heat. Beat in the egg yolks and the crème de menthe. Beat the egg whites until they form stiff peaks, then fold into the chocolate mixture. Spoon into the prepared cases and chill in a refrigerator for at least 1 hour. Decorate each mousse with a chocolate curl before serving.

CRUNCHY CHOCOLATE MOUSSE

Serves 6–8

1 envelope gelatin
4 tablespoons cold water
1½ cups milk
3 eggs, separated
2 tablespoons caster sugar
½ teaspoon vanilla extract
4 oz semisweet chocolate, broken into small pieces

TOPPING
2 tablespoons butter
½ cup fresh brown breadcrumbs
2 tablespoons soft brown sugar

Sprinkle the gelatin over the water in a bowl and leave to soften for 5 minutes. Pour the milk into a pan and bring up to blood temperature. Beat the egg yolks with the sugar and vanilla extract in a bowl or the top of a double boiler until thick and creamy. Pour in the milk. Put over a pan of gently simmering water and cook until the custard has thickened, stirring all the time. Stir in the softened gelatin and, when this has dissolved, add the chocolate, and stir until melted. Remove from the heat and put to one side until the mixture begins to thicken. Stir from time to time.

Beat the egg whites until they form stiff peaks, then fold into the chocolate mixture. Turn into a shallow serving bowl and chill in a refrigerator for at least 1 hour or until set.

To make the topping, melt the butter in a skillet and fry the breadcrumbs until crisp and golden, stirring frequently. Remove from the heat and stir in the sugar. Sprinkle the crumbs over the mousse shortly before serving.

Variation
Spread a layer of whipped cream between the mousse and the fried breadcrumbs.

STRAWBERRY CHOCOLATE BOX

Serves 8

8oz semisweet chocolate, broken into pieces
1 tablespoon vegetable shortening

FILLING
6oz semisweet chocolate, broken into pieces
2 egg yolks
1 tablespoon Kirsch
½ cup heavy cream
½ cup light cream

TOPPING
8oz fresh strawberries, hulled and halved
or quartered
3 tablespoons strawberry jam, sieved
1 tablespoon Kirsch
1oz chocolate, broken into small pieces
½ cup heavy cream

Use either a deep 6 inch square cake pan or a 7 inch square pan about 2 inches deep. Line it with a large piece of heavy duty foil cut in the corners. Ensure that there is enough foil above the top of the pan to pull the set chocolate out (see below).

Melt the chocolate with the vegetable shortening (page 11), pour two-thirds into the pan, then turn and tilt the pan to give an even coating over the sides and base. Allow to set, then repeat with the remaining chocolate and leave to set for about 30 minutes, or until it is quite hard. Remove from the pan by pulling the foil lining carefully. Peel the foil away from the chocolate case gently.

To make the filling, melt the chocolate (page 11), remove from the heat and beat in the egg yolks and Kirsch. Whip together the heavy and light creams until thick, then fold in the chocolate mixture. Pour into the prepared chocolate case and chill in a refrigerator until set.

Arrange the strawberries in the centre of the case, on top of the filling. Put the jam into a small pan, stir in the Kirsch and bring to the boil. Remove from the heat and allow to cool slightly. Spoon the topping over the strawberries; take care not to allow the hot jam to run to the edge of the chocolate case, or it will melt it. Leave for about 5 minutes for the glaze to set. Melt the chocolate (page 11) and allow to cool. Whip the heavy cream until stiff, then beat in the cooled chocolate. Spoon into a pastry bag and pipe neatly round the edge of the case.

POTS AU CHOCOLAT

Serves 6

1 fat vanilla pod
8oz semisweet chocolate, broken into pieces
1 tablespoon confectioners sugar
2 tablespoons butter
3 egg yolks
1 cup heavy cream

DECORATION
2 tablespoons flaked almonds

Using a pointed, sharp knife, split open the vanilla pod and, with a small spoon, scrape out all the moist inside. Melt the chocolate with the confectioners sugar, butter and the inside of the vanilla pod (page 11). Remove from the heat and beat in the egg yolks. Whip the cream until it holds its shape, then beat in the chocolate mixture and beat until thick. Turn into six small ramekins and sprinkle with the almonds. Chill in a refrigerator until ready to serve.

Strawberry Chocolate Box

CHOCOLATE MOUSSE TORTE

Serves 6–8

2 tablespoons dry breadcrumbs
8 oz semisweet chocolate, broken into pieces
1 tablespoon instant coffee granules
4 tablespoons water
8 eggs, separated
¾ cup caster sugar
1 teaspoon vanilla extract

DECORATION
½ cup whipping cream
chocolate curls (page 10)

Lightly butter a 9 inch flan pan or ring (approximately 1 quart capacity) and coat with the dry breadcrumbs. Melt the chocolate with the coffee and water (page 11). Remove from the heat. Beat together the egg yolks, sugar and vanilla extract in a large bowl until thick and creamy, then beat in the chocolate. Beat the egg whites until stiff, then fold into the chocolate mixture. Fill the flan pan with about three-quarters of the mixture. Cover the remainder and chill in a refrigerator.

Bake the flan in a medium oven, 350°F, for 25 minutes. Turn off the oven and leave for a further 5 minutes, then remove and leave to cool for 2 hours.

Fill the cavity in the center with the chilled mixture and chill in a refrigerator for 30 minutes. Whip the cream until stiff and spread over the top. Decorate with the chocolate curls.

RUM AND RAISIN FOOL

Serves 6

⅓ cup raisins
4 tablespoons dark rum
8 oz cold cooked potato
¼ cup caster sugar
7 oz compound chocolate, broken into pieces
1 cup butter
¾ cup heavy cream

Soak the raisins in the rum for about 1 hour. Sieve the potato, then beat in the sugar, raisins and rum.

Melt the chocolate and butter together (page 11). Remove from the heat and beat into the potato mixture. Whip the cream lightly and fold two-thirds of it into the mixture. Turn into a serving dish and chill in a refrigerator for at least 1 hour. Decorate with the remainder of the whipped cream before serving.

AVOCADO FOOL

Serves 4

2 large, ripe avocados, peeled and seeded
juice of 2 limes
2 tablespoons confectioners sugar
2 tablespoons brandy
½ cup heavy cream
3 oz milk chocolate, grated coarsely

Mash the avocados or purée in a blender or food processor with the lime juice and sugar, then add the brandy. Whip the cream until it holds its shape, then fold in the avocado purée. Taste, adding a little extra sugar if necessary, then turn into four individual bowls or glasses. Sprinkle the chocolate over the fools before serving.

CHOCOLATE CREAMS

Serves 6

4 egg yolks
¼ cup caster sugar
½ teaspoon vanilla extract
1 cup heavy cream
1 cup light cream
4 oz semisweet compound chocolate,
broken into pieces
2 tablespoons vegetable oil

DECORATION
whipped cream

Butter six ramekins. Beat the egg yolks lightly with the sugar and vanilla extract. Mix together the heavy and light creams and heat to blood temperature. Beat into the egg yolks.

Turn the mixture into the prepared ramekins, cover with foil and stand in a roasting pan containing 1 inch cold water. Bake in a warm oven, 325°F, for about 30 minutes, or until set. Remove from the oven, take out of the water and leave to cool for about 1 hour.

Melt the chocolate with the oil (page 11); this makes it softer for serving. Spoon over the creams, then chill for at least 6 hours. Top each cream with a spoonful of whipped cream before serving.

APRICOT FRUIT BASKET

Serves 6–8

7 oz milk chocolate **or** milk compound
chocolate, broken into pieces
1½ lb fresh apricots, halved and pitted
1 oz sugar
4 tablespoons white wine
1 cup heavy cream

Melt the chocolate (page 11), and use all but about 3 tablespoons to coat evenly the inside of a 9×5 inch foil container 2 inches deep; use about a third of the melted chocolate at a time, so that it sets quickly. Leave to set in a cool place for at least 30 minutes.

Use the remainder of the chocolate to make a handle. Draw a circle, about ½ inch smaller than the width of the foil dish, on a piece of waxed paper or non-stick silicon paper. Spoon the chocolate either into a wax paper pastry bag or into a nylon pastry bag fitted with a small writing tip. Use to pipe a simple trellis pattern round the circle; the easiest one is one wavy line followed by a second wavy line in the opposite direction on top. Leave to set, then carefully cut into two semi-circles, using a sharp knife. Brush the smooth side of one of these with the chocolate remaining in the bowl (you only need a very little), then place the second semi-circle on top, again smooth side down. Leave to set.

Put half the apricots into a blender or food processor, and purée with the sugar and white wine. Whip the cream until it just holds its shape, then carefully fold in the apricot purée.

When the chocolate in the container is quite hard, loosen the foil very gently, and peel away from the chocolate. Spoon the apricot fool into the chocolate case. Arrange the remaining apricot halves on the top, piling them up to look like fruit in a basket. Place the handle in position, pressing it gently into the fool. Decorate with fruit leaves, if liked.

Tia Maria Soufflé

Serves 6

1 envelope powdered gelatin
4 tablespoons cold water
1½ cups milk
3 eggs, separated
¼ cup caster sugar
1 teaspoon vanilla extract
2 tablespoons flour, sifted
8 oz semisweet chocolate, broken into small pieces
4 tablespoons Tia Maria
1 cup whipping cream

DECORATION
whipped cream
chocolate leaves **or** horns (page 10)

Make a collar for a 1½ pint soufflé dish, using a piece of double wax or non-stick silicon paper; the collar should stand at least 4 inches above the rim of the soufflé dish. Brush one side of the piece of paper with oil or butter, wrap round the soufflé dish, the greased side facing inwards, and tie in position with string.

Sprinkle the gelatin over the water in a bowl and leave to soften for 5 minutes. Pour the milk into a pan and bring to the boil. Beat the egg yolks lightly with the sugar and vanilla extract, then beat in the flour. Pour over the boiling milk, stirring well. Return the mixture to the pan and bring to the boil, stirring all the time, then cook for 2–3 minutes. Remove from the heat and stir in the softened gelatin; leave until dissolved. Add the chocolate and stir until melted. Stir in the Tia Maria. Cover with clingfilm and leave to cool.

Whip the cream until it forms soft peaks, then beat the egg whites until stiff. Fold, first, the cream and then the egg whites into the chocolate custard. Turn the mixture into the prepared dish. Chill in a refrigerator for at least 2 hours.

Before serving, peel off the paper collar carefully, easing it off with a knife. Decorate the top of the soufflé with piped cream and chocolate leaves or horns.

Chocolate Chestnut Soufflé

Serves 6–8

1 lb chestnuts
¾ cup milk
¼ cup sugar
6 oz bittersweet chocolate, broken into small pieces
2 tablespoons brandy
4 eggs, separated
¾ cup heavy cream

DECORATION
marrons glacé

Make a slit in each chestnut with a sharp knife and cook in boiling water for 5 minutes, then peel off the shells. The chestnuts must be left in hot water until they are to be peeled. If you find the brown skins are becoming difficult to peel off, the pan should be replaced on the heat.

Place the chestnuts in a pan with the milk and sugar, and simmer gently for 20 minutes or until tender. Either sieve the chestnuts or purée in a blender or food processor. Replace the chestnut purée in the pan and put over gentle heat. When almost boiling, remove from the heat and stir in the chocolate. Stir until the chocolate has melted, then beat in, first the brandy and then the egg yolks, one at a time. Lightly whip the cream and beat the egg whites until stiff. Fold, first, the cream and then the egg whites into the chocolate mixture. Turn into a serving dish and chill until required. Decorate with marrons glacé before serving.

Variation
Use 14 oz canned sweetened chestnut purée in place of the fresh chestnuts, milk and sugar.

Tia Maria Soufflé **and** *Avocado Fool (page 50)*

CHOCOLATE AND PINEAPPLE ROULADE

Serves 6–8

4 eggs, separated
10 tablespoons caster sugar
¼ teaspoon vanilla extract
⅓ cup cocoa powder

FILLING AND DECORATION
1 cup heavy cream
1 lb pineapple pieces, fresh **or** canned and drained
chocolate vermicelli

Grease and line a 13×9 inch jelly roll pan. Beat the egg yolks, sugar and vanilla extract until thick and creamy. Beat the egg whites until they form stiff peaks. Fold the cocoa into the egg yolks. Stir in 1 tablespoon of the beaten egg white. Fold in the remainder of the egg white.

Turn the mixture into the prepared pan and spread evenly. Bake in a medium oven, 350°F, for 15 minutes or until just cooked. Do not over-cook or the roll will crack more easily. Remove from the oven, cover with a clean dish-towel and leave until quite cold. Invert on to a piece of wax paper dredged with caster sugar, and peel off the paper carefully.

To make the filling, whip the cream until stiff. Reserve a few pieces of the pineapple for decoration and mix the remaining pineapple with two-thirds of the cream. Spread evenly all over the roulade, then roll it up, pushing it along the wax paper. Place on a serving plate. Pipe the remaining cream along the top to decorate, and top with the remaining pieces of pineapple and the chocolate vermicelli.

Note Do not worry if the roulade cracks slightly when you roll it up as you can always mask the cracks with cream or sprinkle confectioners sugar over them.

BAVAROIS AU CHOCOLAT

Serves 6–8

1 envelope powdered gelatin
4 tablespoons cold water
4 egg yolks
¼ cup caster sugar
1 teaspoon vanilla extract
2 cups milk
8 oz semisweet chocolate, broken into small pieces
½ cup heavy cream
½ cup light cream

DECORATION
chocolate curls (page 10) **or** whipped cream

Oil a 1½ quart mold lightly or dampen with cold water. Sprinkle the gelatin over the water in a bowl and leave to soften for about 5 minutes. Beat together the egg yolks, sugar and vanilla extract for 5 minutes. Warm the milk and stir into the egg yolks and sugar. Blend well and put into the top of a double boiler, or into a bowl placed over a pan of gently simmering water. Cook gently, stirring all the time, until the mixture thickens. Stir in the softened gelatin and, when this has dissolved, add the chocolate. Stir until the chocolate has melted. Remove from the heat, put into a cold place and leave until the mixture begins to thicken. Whip the heavy and light creams lightly and fold into the mixture when it is thick but not set. Turn into the prepared mold and chill for at least 2 hours or until set.

To turn out, dip the mold into boiling water (see **Note**). Invert on to a plate and remove the mold. Decorate with chocolate curls or whipped cream.

Note If using a tin mold, dip for 3–4 seconds. If using a china mold, about 15 seconds will be required.

CHOCOLATE AND ALMOND LAYER PUDDING

Serves 4–6

2 oz semisweet chocolate, broken into pieces
¼ cup unsalted butter
⅓ cup caster sugar
a few drops vanilla extract
½ cup ground almonds
juice of ½ lemon

TOPPING

1 oz semisweet chocolate, broken into pieces
2 tablespoons butter
½ cup heavy cream

Melt the chocolate (page 11) and cool slightly. Cream the butter, beat in 2 tablespoons sugar and the vanilla extract. Beat until smooth and fluffy, then beat in the chocolate. Turn into a small glass serving bowl and spread evenly. Chill for at least 30 minutes. Mix the almonds with the remaining sugar and lemon juice and spread evenly over the chocolate mixture. Chill while preparing the topping.

Melt the chocolate with the butter (page 11) and remove from the heat. Whip the cream lightly and fold gently into the chocolate. Spoon the topping over the chilled mixture, forming the cream into swirls. Chill in a refrigerator until ready to serve.

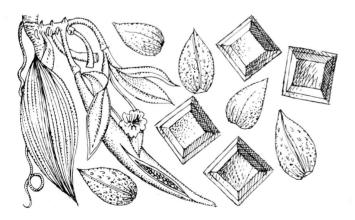

CHOCOLATE CHIFFON PIE

Serves 4–6

1½ cups flour
a pinch of salt
½ cup butter **or** margarine
cold water

FILLING AND TOPPING

1 envelope powdered gelatin
2 tablespoons cold water
3 eggs, separated
¼ cup caster sugar
4 oz semisweet compound chocolate,
broken into pieces
1 tablespoon cocoa powder
1 teaspoon instant coffee granules
½ cup whipping cream

Sift together the flour and salt. Rub in the butter or margarine until the mixture resembles fine breadcrumbs, then bind with cold water to make a firm dough. Turn on to a floured surface and knead lightly. Roll out and use to line an 8 inch pie plate or pan. Prebake in a medium hot oven, 375°F, for 20–25 minutes. Leave to cool.

To make the filling, sprinkle the gelatin over the cold water in a bowl. Leave to soften for 5 minutes. Put the egg yolks and sugar into the top of a double boiler or a bowl over a pan of boiling water, and beat until the mixture thickens. Beat in the gelatin and stir until dissolved. Stir in the chocolate, cocoa and coffee granules. Continue stirring until the chocolate has melted. Remove from the heat and allow to cool slightly. Beat the egg whites until they form stiff peaks, then fold into the chocolate mixture.

Turn the mixture into the baked tart shell and chill in a refrigerator for at least 1 hour. Before serving, whip the cream lightly, and spread over the top of the pie.

MARBLED SAVARIN

Serves 12

¾ cup butter
1 cup milk
1 teaspoon sugar
2½ teaspoons dried yeast
2¾ cups flour
a pinch of salt
3 eggs, beaten
¼ cup cocoa powder

SYRUP AND FILLING
3 cups sugar
2 cups water
½ cup dark rum
2 lb prepared fresh fruit in season

Grease and flour a 9 inch ring pan. Melt the butter in a pan, then leave to cool. Heat the milk to blood temperature, then pour into a bowl. Stir in the sugar and sprinkle with the yeast. Leave in a warm place for 10 minutes or until frothy. Sift together 2 cups of the flour with the salt into a mixing bowl. Make a hollow in the center, pour in the yeast mixture and the eggs, and mix well with a wooden spoon to make a smooth dough. Beat in the cooled butter, and beat for a further 2–3 minutes. Divide the mixture in half. Sift the remaining flour into one half and the cocoa into the other half. Beat both batters until smooth.

Put alternate spoonfuls of the mixtures into the prepared pan. Cover with a piece of oiled clingfilm and put into a warm place for about 40 minutes, or until the dough has risen almost to the top of the pan. Bake in a hot oven, 425°F, for about 25 minutes, or until golden-brown and firm. Cool in the pan for 5 minutes, then turn out on to a wire rack with a plate underneath.

Make the syrup while the savarin is cooking. Put the sugar into a pan with the water and stir over low heat until the sugar has dissolved. Bring to the boil, then remove from the heat and stir in the rum.

While the savarin is still hot, prick it all over with a fine skewer and pour over the warm rum syrup, a little at a time. When all the syrup has been used, pour any which has drained on to the plate back into the pan. Pour over the savarin again. Repeat until only about ½ cup is left. Carefully place the savarin on a serving plate. Mix the remaining syrup with the fruit, and spoon this into the center of the savarin.

Serve with whipped cream.

SAINT EMILION AU CHOCOLAT

Serves 6–8

12–16 macaroons
4 tablespoons dark rum
½ cup butter
¾ cup caster sugar
½ cup milk
1 egg
8 oz semisweet chocolate, broken into pieces

Put the macaroons on to a serving plate and sprinkle lightly with the rum. Cream together the butter and sugar until light and fluffy. Put the milk into a pan and bring to the boil. Remove from the heat, leave for about 10 minutes to cool, then beat in the egg.

Melt the chocolate (page 11) and, leaving it over the heat, beat in the milk, then the butter and sugar. Continue to beat until very smooth.

Put four of the macaroons into the bottom of a serving bowl. Pour over half the chocolate sauce. Repeat with four more macaroons and the rest of the chocolate sauce. Top with the remaining macaroons. Chill in a refrigerator for at least 12 hours.

Saint Emilion au Chocolat

CRACKOLATE CHEESECAKE

Serves 6–8

¼ cup butter
2 tablespoons golden syrup
2 tablespoons granulated sugar
2 tablespoons cocoa powder
¾ cup rice krispies

FILLING
¾ lb strawberries, hulled
¾ lb cottage cheese
1 envelope powdered gelatin
4 tablespoons cold water
2 eggs, separated
⅓ cup caster sugar
grated rind of 1 lemon
½ cup whipping cream

DECORATION
½ cup whipping cream
chocolate leaves (page 10)

Lightly oil a loose-bottomed 8 inch cake pan. Put the butter, syrup, sugar and cocoa into a pan and stir over low heat until the butter has melted and the sugar dissolved. Remove from the heat and stir in the rice krispies. Spread evenly over the bottom of the prepared pan and leave to set for 30 minutes.

To make the filling, rub the strawberries with the cottage cheese through a sieve, or purée in a blender or food processor. Sprinkle the gelatin over the cold water in a bowl and leave to soften for 5 minutes. Stand over a pan of simmering water and leave until the gelatin has dissolved. Remove from the heat and cool slightly. Beat the yolks with the sugar and lemon rind until thick and creamy. Beat the whites until stiff. Whip the cream until stiff. Stir the strawberry and cheese purée into the egg yolk mixture, stir in the gelatin, then fold in the cream and finally the egg whites. Turn into the prepared pan on top of the chocolate base and leave to set for at least 2 hours.

To serve, carefully push the cake out of the pan from the base. Loosen the base with a spatula and transfer to a serving plate. Whip the cream, and spread evenly over the top of the cake. Decorate with the chocolate leaves.

CHOCOLATE AND GINGER CHEESECAKE

Serves 6

7 oz ginger cookies
⅓ cup butter
1 tablespoon Demerara sugar

FILLING
4 oz semisweet chocolate, broken into pieces
½ lb cream cheese
2 tablespoons ginger syrup
3 tablespoons light cream
2 eggs, separated
3 pieces preserved stem ginger, chopped finely

DECORATION
4 tablespoons whipped cream (approx)
1–2 pieces preserved stem ginger, sliced

Crush the cookies with a rolling-pin between the folds of a dish-towel, or use a food processor. Melt the butter in a small pan, remove from the heat and stir in the cookies and sugar. Press into a 8–9 inch flan pan or dish, and chill.

To make the filling, melt the chocolate (page 11). Remove from the heat. Beat the cream cheese with the ginger syrup and light cream, then beat in the egg yolks, one at a time, followed by the chocolate and ginger. Beat the egg whites until stiff, then fold into the cream cheese mixture.

Turn the mixture into the cookie cases and chill in a refrigerator for at least 1 hour. Decorate with whipped cream, piped or swirled on the top, and small pieces of stem ginger.

Hazelnut and Orange Torte

Serves 6–8

2 eggs, separated
¾ cup caster sugar
3 oz semisweet chocolate, broken into pieces
½ cup butter
½ cup hazelnuts, chopped
2 tablespoons Cointreau
½ cup orange juice
24 ladyfingers
½ cup heavy cream

Oil a cookie sheet lightly and line with non-stick silicon paper. Beat the egg whites until stiff, then beat in ½ cup of the sugar, 1 teaspoon at a time, until the mixture is stiff and shiny. Put in a pastry bag fitted with a large rose tip, and pipe small meringues, about 1½ inches in diameter, to make about 20. Bake in a very cool oven, 250°F, for about 2 hours or until the meringues are crisp. Remove from the oven and leave to cool.

Butter a 900g/2 lb loaf tin lightly and line with non-stick silicon paper. Melt the chocolate (page 11), remove from the heat and cool slightly. Cream together the butter and remaining sugar until light and fluffy, then beat in the chocolate and hazelnuts. Mix the Cointreau with the orange juice. Dip each ladyfinger into the orange mixture for a few seconds, then arrange one-third of them on the base of the pan, sugar side outwards. Spread with half the chocolate mixture. Repeat for the next layer, and finish with a layer of ladyfingers. Cover with a piece of foil, and place a weight on top. Chill in a refrigerator for at least 2 hours, then remove from the pan. Whip the cream until stiff and spread over the cake. Decorate with the meringues.

Hazelnut Meringue Gâteau

Serves 6–8

⅓ cup hazelnuts
3 egg whites
½ cup caster sugar

FILLING
1 oz semisweet chocolate
1 tablespoon cocoa powder
1 tablespoon hot water
⅓ cup unsalted butter
¾ cup confectioners sugar, sifted
¾ cup whipping cream

Grease and line two 6½–7 inch layer-cake pans. Chop the nuts very finely or grind in a blender or food processor (they should not be as fine as ground almonds, however, but more like coarse breadcrumbs). Whip the egg whites until they form stiff peaks, then beat in the sugar, 1 teaspoon at a time until the mixture is stiff and shiny. Fold in the hazelnuts. Divide the mixture between the prepared pans, spreading it evenly. Bake in a moderately hot oven, 375°F, for 20 minutes. Turn off the heat and leave to cool in the oven. Remove from the pans carefully.

To make the filling, melt the chocolate (page 11). Blend the cocoa powder with the hot, not boiling, water. Cream the butter, then gradually beat in the confectioners sugar. Beat in the chocolate and the cocoa powder mixture. Spread this over one of the cakes. Whip the cream until stiff and spread half over the chocolate mixture. Sandwich the cakes together and decorate the top with the remaining cream piped or swirled over it.

BLACK FOREST MERINGUE

Serves 8–10

4 egg whites
1 cup caster sugar

FILLING AND DECORATION
1½lb jar Morello cherries
1 tablespoon arrowroot
5 tablespoons Kirsch
1½ cups heavy cream
¾ cup light cream
6oz semisweet chocolate, coarsely grated
chocolate leaves (page 10)

Draw two circles, about 8–9 inches in diameter, on two pieces of non-stick silicon paper. Oil both sides and place on two cookie trays. Whip the egg whites until stiff, then beat in the sugar, 1 teaspoon at a time, until the meringue is stiff and shiny. Divide the mixture between the two circles and spread evenly. Bake in a very cool oven, 250°F, for about 4 hours or until quite dry. Remove from the oven and leave to cool, then peel off the paper carefully.

To make the filling, drain the cherries, and pit all but a few of them; reserve these for decoration. Blend the arrowroot with 3 tablespoons of the cherry syrup. Heat the remainder of the syrup to just below boiling point, then pour over the blended arrowroot. Return to the pan and bring back to the boil, stirring all the time, until thickened. Remove from the heat and stir in the pitted cherries, then stir in 2 tablespoons of the Kirsch. Leave to cool.

Whip the heavy and light creams together until they hold their shape. Whip the remaining Kirsch into the cream and then fold in the grated chocolate.

Spread a layer of cream over one of the meringue circles, then carefully spoon the pitted cherries and sauce evenly over the top. Place the second meringue on top, but place it with the underside (ie the smooth side) uppermost. Spread the remaining cream all over the top and sides of the meringue. Lift carefully on to a serving plate and decorate the top with the reserved cherries and the chocolate leaves. Chill for at least 1 hour before serving to allow the meringue to soften slightly and the chocolate to infuse into the cream.

MOCHA ICE CREAM

Serves 6

½ cup soft brown sugar
4 tablespoons cocoa powder
2 tablespoons instant coffee granules
¼ cup butter
5 tablespoons water
2 cups canned evaporated milk

Put the sugar, cocoa, coffee, butter and water into a pan. Heat gently, stirring until melted, then bring to the boil. Leave to cool. Pour the evaporated milk into a large mixing bowl. Beat until thick and frothy and the beater leaves a trail, then beat in the cooled sauce until well blended.

Turn the mixture into a freezer and leave until partially frozen. Remove and beat well. Pour into a freezer container, freeze until firm, then cover.

CHOCOLATE CHIP BROWN BREAD ICE CREAM

Serves 6

1 cup heavy cream
½ cup light cream
2 eggs, separated
½ cup confectioners sugar, sifted
1 cup wholewheat breadcrumbs
2oz semisweet chocolate, grated coarsely
or chopped finely

Lightly whip the heavy and light creams together until they hold their shape. Beat the yolks and confectioners sugar until thick and creamy, then stir in the breadcrumbs and chocolate. Fold into the whipped cream. Beat the whites until they form stiff peaks, then fold into the cream. Turn the mixture into a 1 quart freezer container and freeze for 2–3 hours until firm.

Marbled Ice (page 62), Mocha Ice Cream **and** *Chocolate Chip Brown Bread Ice Cream*

MARBLED ICE

Serves 6–8

1 cup milk
⅓ cup caster sugar
4 egg yolks
1 cup heavy cream
½ teaspoon vanilla extract
3 oz semisweet chocolate, broken into pieces

Heat the milk with the sugar to blood temperature. Beat the egg yolks, then pour over the hot milk, beating all the time. Return the mixture to the pan and stir over very low heat until the custard thickens; take great care not to curdle the mixture. Remove from the heat, cover the pan with clingfilm and leave to cool.

Whip the cream very lightly; it should be just slightly thickened. Beat the cooled custard and fold into the cream. Pour half the mixture into a plastic container and stir in the vanilla extract.

Melt the chocolate (page 11), and stir into the remaining mixture. Carefully pour the chocolate mixture in a zig-zag pattern over the vanilla ice. Stir very lightly with a spoon to give a marbled appearance. Freeze for at least 4 hours.

LA DAME BLANCHE

Serves 4

1 cup vanilla ice cream
4 meringue shells
cold Rich Chocolate Sauce (1) (page 75)

CRÈME CHANTILLY
½ cup heavy cream
1 egg white
1 tablespoon confectioners sugar, sifted

Make the crème chantilly first. Whip the cream until it holds its shape. Beat the egg white until stiff, then beat in the confectioners sugar, 1 teaspoon at a time. Fold into the cream.

Put two scoops of ice cream on each serving plate. Top with a meringue shell, then pour over a quarter of the chocolate sauce and top with a quarter of the crème chantilly. Serve at once.

FROSTY STRAWBERRY LAYER

Serves 4–6

½ cup flour
1 tablespoon cocoa powder
¼ cup butter
¼ cup soft brown sugar
2 tablespoons chopped hazelnuts

STRAWBERRY LAYER
1 egg white
1 tablespoon lemon juice
½ lb fresh **or** frozen strawberries, thawed
½ cup caster sugar
¾ cup whipping cream

Sift together the flour and cocoa into a bowl. Melt the butter in a pan. Add the sugar, nuts and butter to the flour, and mix together. Spread evenly over the base of a 7 inch layer-cake pan and bake in a medium oven, 350°F, for 15 minutes, or until crisp. Remove from the oven, leave to cool, then break into crumbs with your fingers.

To make the strawberry layer, put the egg white, lemon juice, strawberries and sugar into a large bowl. Beat with an electric beater at low speed. When the mixture starts to thicken, beat at high speed for about 10 minutes or until it forms stiff peaks. Whip the cream lightly and fold into the strawberry mixture.

Spoon half the strawberry mixture into the base of a freezer-proof dish, sprinkle with half the crumbs, then cover with the remaining strawberry mixture, and top with the last of the crumbs. Freeze for at least 6 hours. Serve from the dish.

Chocolate Terrine with Cherry Sauce

Terrine serves 12–16
Sauce serves 8–10

½ lb semisweet chocolate, broken into pieces
1 cup unsalted butter
½ cup confectioners sugar
½ cup cocoa powder
4 egg yolks
½ cup granulated sugar
½ cup water
1 cup heavy cream
1 cup pitted black cherries
(fresh **or** frozen), chopped roughly

SAUCE
1 lb pitted black cherries
(fresh **or** frozen)
1¼ cups water
½ cup sugar
2 tablespoons cornstarch
4 tablespoons Kirsch (optional)

Butter a 3 lb loaf pan. Melt the chocolate (page 11). Remove from the heat and leave to cool slightly. Cream the butter until light and fluffy. Sift the confectioners sugar and cocoa together and beat into the butter alternately with the chocolate. Beat the yolks lightly in a separate bowl. Put the sugar and water into a small, heavy-based pan and stir over low heat until the sugar has dissolved. Boil rapidly to 225°F on a candy thermometer (thread stage). Beat into the yolks, a little at a time, and beat to a mousse-like consistency. Beat slowly into the butter mixture. Whip the cream lightly, then fold into the chocolate mixture. Fold in the cherries last. Turn into the prepared pan and freeze for 6 hours or until firm. Serve each portion with about 2 tablespoons of hot cherry sauce.

To make the cherry sauce, put the cherries, all but 3 tablespoons of the water and the sugar into a pan, and bring to the boil. Blend the cornstarch with the remaining water, stir into the pan and bring back to the boil, stirring all the time. Remove from the heat and stir in the Kirsch, if used.

Layered Log Ice Cream

Serves 8

2 teaspoons instant coffee granules
1 tablespoon Tia Maria **or** rum
½ cup hazelnuts
½ cup shredded coconut
1 heaping tablespoon chocolate spread
1 tablespoon milk **or** coconut milk
2 quarts vanilla ice cream
3 oz semisweet chocolate, broken into pieces

Dissolve the coffee in the Tia Maria or rum. Toast the hazelnuts under a moderate broiler for a few minutes. Remove from the heat and, when cool enough to handle, rub them together until the skins come off. Replace the nuts under the broiler and cook until golden-brown, taking care that they do not burn, then chop them very finely by hand or with a blender or food processor.

Lightly toast the coconut, making sure it all becomes evenly golden and does not burn. Blend the chocolate spread with the milk or coconut milk to form a smooth paste.

Divide the ice cream into three portions; leave two in the freezer and place the third in a mixing bowl. Chop this roughly into about six portions and leave to soften for about 5 minutes. Pour in the coffee mixture, then beat well (preferably with an electric beater). Turn into a 2 lb loaf pan, spread evenly over the base, then replace in the freezer for about 10 minutes until quite firm.

Remove a second portion of ice cream, chop and soften as before and beat in the hazelnuts. Spread this over the coffee ice cream and leave to harden in the freezer.

Finally, beat the chocolate spread and coconut milk into the last portion of ice cream, spread over the hazelnut mixture and freeze for at least 1 hour.

To turn the ice cream out, quickly dip the pan into a bowl of very hot water for a few seconds, and invert on to a plate. Replace in the freezer for 5 minutes. Melt the chocolate and drizzle all over the top and sides of the ice cream (page 10). Replace in the freezer until ready to serve.

CHOCOLATE AND STRAWBERRY BOMBE

Serves 8

CHOCOLATE ICE CREAM
4 egg yolks
⅓ cup caster sugar
2 cups light cream
3 oz semisweet chocolate, broken into small pieces

STRAWBERRY ICE CREAM
¾ lb fresh **or** frozen strawberries, thawed
4 egg yolks
½ cup caster sugar
1½ cups light cream

DECORATION (optional)
fresh strawberries

Beat the egg yolks and sugar in a bowl over a pan of simmering water until thick and creamy. Heat the cream in a small pan to blood temperature. Stir into the egg yolks and cook over low heat, stirring all the time, until the mixture thickens. Remove from the heat and stir in the chocolate until melted. Pour into a 1½ quart bowl and leave to cool for about 1 hour. Put a 1½ pint bowl in the center and place enough weights inside to bring the mixture level with the top of the bowl. Freeze for at least 2 hours or until firm.

Pour a little hot water into the inner bowl, and as soon as the ice cream round the edge starts to melt, remove it carefully. Return the ice cream to the freezer.

To make the strawberry ice cream, rub the strawberries through a sieve or purée in a blender or food processor. Using the egg yolks, sugar and cream, make the ice cream mixture as for the chocolate ice cream. Remove from the heat and stir in the strawberry purée. Cool for about 1 hour. Pour the strawberry ice cream into the cavity left in the center of the chocolate ice cream, and freeze for a further 2–3 hours until quite firm.

To turn out, quickly dip the bowl into a bowl of very hot water for a few seconds and invert on to a serving plate. Either serve the bombe as it is, or decorate with fresh strawberries.

CHOCOLATE TUTTI FRUTTI BOMBE

Serves 8–12

½ lb compound chocolate,
broken into pieces
3 eggs, separated
½ cup confectioners sugar, sifted
1 cup heavy cream
1 cup candied cherries, chopped
1 cup dried apricots, chopped
1 cup candied peel, chopped
1 cup blanched almonds, chopped
5 tablespoons brandy **or** dark rum

Put a 2 quart dessert bowl (a plastic one is ideal) in the freezer for a few minutes. Melt the chocolate (page 11). Remove the bowl and pour in the chocolate. Roll it round and round until the inside is coated evenly. Leave to set.

Beat the egg yolks with 2 tablespoons of the sugar until thick and creamy. Beat the egg whites until stiff, then beat in the remaining sugar, 1 teaspoon at a time. Beat in the egg yolks gradually. Whip the cream lightly. Fold all the fruit and nuts into the egg mixture, then fold in the cream. Turn the mixture into the prepared bowl. If the ice cream level does not quite reach the level of the chocolate, neaten off with a sharp knife. Any excess chocolate can be chopped and stirred into the ice cream mixture. Cover the bowl and freeze for at least 4 hours or until quite firm.

To turn the dessert out, dip into a bowl of very hot water for about 1 minute and invert on to a plate; replace in the freezer. About 30 minutes before serving, place on a serving plate and put in the refrigerator; (do not use the plate that has been in the freezer as this will prevent the alcohol from igniting.)

Put the brandy or rum into a small pan and heat gently, then pour over the dessert, and ignite.

Note It does not matter if the chocolate covering is not smoothly coated, as it will not be visible once the bombe is filled with ice cream.

Chocolate and Strawberry Bombe

LEMON SORBET WITH RASPBERRY SAUCE

Serves 6

1 pint carton lemon sorbet
6oz semisweet chocolate, broken into pieces
2 tablespoons vegetable oil
¾lb frozen raspberries, thawed
¼ cup confectioners sugar

Using either a small ice-cream scoop or a dessert-spoon, form the sorbet into 18 balls. Place on a piece of non-stick silicon or wax paper on a tray and put into a freezer for about 10 minutes to harden.

Melt the chocolate with the oil (page 11) and allow to cool slightly. Spoon a little chocolate carefully over each ball of sorbet, coating them evenly. Return the tray to the freezer for at least 15 minutes.

Reserve six raspberries for decoration. Rub the remaining raspberries through a sieve or purée in a blender or food processor (then sieve the purée to remove the seeds). Stir in the confectioners sugar. To serve, divide the sauce between six plates, top with three balls of chocolate-covered sorbet and decorate each one with a raspberry.

Variation
Different flavors of sorbet, and combinations of flavors, can be used.

TROPICAL SURPRISE

Serves 8

8 small sponge cakes
1 cup tropical fruit juice,
ie a mixture of passion fruit, pineapple, orange juice, etc.
If this is not available, use orange juice
1 pint chocolate ice cream
1 cup whipping cream, whipped lightly

DECORATION
1oz semisweet chocolate, grated

Dip four of the sponge cakes in the fruit juice and place on a rectangular serving dish. Place the ice cream on top, dip the remaining sponge cakes in the fruit juice and place on top of the ice cream. Flatten out slightly. Whip the cream lightly, and use to cover the ice cream and sponge. Decorate with the grated chocolate.

Note   If this dessert is not to be served immediately, put it into a freezer or the freezing compartment of a refrigerator for 15 minutes, then transfer to a refrigerator for up to 30 minutes. Do not prepare more than 45 minutes in advance.

MAKING CHOCOLATE CANDIES

What present could be more appreciated than a pretty box of home-made chocolate candies? An old-fashioned term, perhaps, but the great thing is that they are fun to make, and generally much cheaper than bought ones. It is easy to make them look attractive in paper candy cases, arranged carefully in a box or jar and tied with ribbon. And to end your dinner party in style, impress your guests with a bowl of home-made chocolate-covered mints or delicious truffles.

All the recipes here are very straightforward, but once you have mastered them you are sure to go on and experiment with more complicated ideas. While no detailed confectionery knowledge is required, it is, nevertheless, necessary to know how to recognize the different temperatures used when boiling sugar (see chart below). If you progress to making fudge and toffee regularly, it is well worth investing in a candy thermometer as this is an easy and quick way of checking the temperature.

SUGAR BOILING TEMPERATURES

Temperatures	Name of Test	Method of Testing
215–225°F	Thread	Dip the handles of two wooden spoons first into some oil and then into the boiling sugar syrup. The syrup should form into a fine thread when pulled apart.
240°F	Soft Ball	A little of the syrup can be rolled into a soft ball in your fingers when poured into a cup of cold water.
250°F	Hard Ball	The mixture forms a larger, harder ball than obtained with the Soft Ball test above.
280°F	Soft Crack	A few drops of the syrup poured into a bowl of cold water soon becomes brittle and a thin piece will snap.
310°F	Hard Crack	Test as for the Soft Crack, but the syrup becomes very brittle.
345°F	Caramel	The sugar changes to a pale golden-brown and the longer it is boiled, the darker it becomes.

EASTER EGGS

Making Easter Eggs at home not only saves money, but provides amusement for all the family, especially for children who will not find it at all difficult, especially if you use compound chocolate.

Plastic and metal molds can be obtained from most good gourmet shops. Make sure they are dry and clean, and polish them well with a piece of paper toweling before you set to work. Do not grease the molds. Melt the chocolate (page 11) and spoon some into the mold, tilting it to coat the inside completely. If you have too much, pour it out before it sets; if you have too little, quickly spoon in some more.

Place the mold upside-down on a sheet of wax paper and leave it in a cold place to set (not a refrigerator). When the first layer of chocolate is hard, you can add another one; this will make the egg easier to unmold, but it is not vital.

When the chocolate is hard and has shrunk away from the edges of the mold a little, ease it out gently with a spatula.

Fill the Easter egg with candies and chocolates if you like, and join the two halves by brushing the rims with melted chocolate and pressing them gently together.

Note Remember that any casualties which break when removed from the mold, can be re-melted and used again.

CHOCOLATE DIPPED FRUITS

These provide attractive, quickly made petits fours. A variety of different fruits are suitable, from strawberries and grapes to cherries, peeled lychees and mandarin sections. Choose ripe but firm fruit, free from any blemish. If the fruit has a stem, such as a cherry, leave it on. Make sure the fruit is clean and dry, and dip each one in melted chocolate (page 11), holding it by the stem if it has one, otherwise using a toothpick. Place on wax or non-stick paper and leave in a cool place to dry. When the chocolate has set, put the dipped fruit in petits fours cases. Do not store for more than 24 hours; they are at their best up to 12 hours after the chocolate has set.

A Selection of Sweetmeats
Easter Eggs, Chocolate Dipped Fruit, Fruit and Nut Clusters (page 73), Chocolate Cream Truffles (page 70), Colettes (page 70), Chocolate Peppermint Creams (page 72) **and** *Walnut Mocha Fudge (page 71)*

CHOCOLATE CREAM TRUFFLES

Makes 24

4 oz milk chocolate, broken into pieces
4 tablespoons double cream
¼ teaspoon vanilla extract
2½ cups confectioners sugar, sifted
2 tablespoons extra confectioners sugar
¼ teaspoon ground cinnamon

Melt the chocolate (page 11), then stir in the cream and vanilla extract. Remove from the heat and gradually beat in 2½ cups of the confectioners sugar to give a firm paste. Divide into 24 pieces and shape into balls.

Sift the remaining confectioners sugar with the cinnamon on to a sheet of wax paper. Roll the truffles in the spiced sugar until completely coated, then place in paper candy cases.

RICH CHOCOLATE TRUFFLES

Makes 24

4 oz semisweet chocolate, broken into small pieces
1 tablespoon liqueur,
eg Grand Marnier, Cointreau, Tia Maria, etc
2 cups confectioners sugar, sifted
½ cup unsalted butter
2 tablespoons instant chocolate milk mix

Melt the chocolate (page 11). Remove from the heat and beat in the liqueur, confectioners sugar and butter until smooth. If necessary, add a little more confectioners sugar to give a firm paste. Divide into 24 pieces and shape into balls. Roll each one in the instant chocolate milk mix until completely covered, then place in paper candy cases.

CHOCOLATE RUM TRUFFLES

Makes 24

4 oz semisweet chocolate, broken into small pieces
1 tablespoon dark rum
2 tablespoons unsalted butter
1 egg yolk
1 cup ground almonds
1 cup cake crumbs
¼ cup chocolate **or** colored vermicelli

Melt the chocolate with the rum (page 11). Beat in the butter and egg yolk, then remove from the heat. Stir in the ground almonds and cake crumbs to make a smooth firm paste. Divide into 24 pieces and shape into balls. Roll in the vermicelli until completely covered, then place in paper candy cases.

COLETTES

Makes 18

8 oz semisweet chocolate, broken into small pieces
4 tablespoons water
1 tablespoon strong black coffee
¼ cup butter
2 egg yolks
1 teaspoon dark rum

Melt 4 oz of the chocolate (page 11). Remove from the heat and put a good teaspoonful into 18 waxed paper candy cases. Using the handle of a teaspoon, spread evenly round the base and sides of each case. Leave to set in a cool place.

Put the remaining chocolate into a small pan with the water and coffee. Stir over very low heat until the chocolate has melted, then boil for 2 minutes, stirring frequently. Remove the pan from the heat and allow the mixture to cool. Beat in the butter, a little at a time, then blend in the egg yolks and the rum. Leave in a cold place until thickened.

When the chocolate cases have set, peel off the paper candy cases carefully. Spoon the filling into a pastry bag fitted with a ½ inch rose tip and pipe into each chocolate case.

CHOCOLATE WHIRLS

Makes 18

¼ cup soft brown sugar
2 egg yolks
½ cup light cream
7oz semisweet chocolate, broken into small pieces

Put the sugar and egg yolks in a mixing bowl over a pan of hot, not boiling, water. Beat together until pale and thick. Blend in the cream and continue to cook, stirring until the custard coats the back of a spoon. Turn off the heat, but leave the bowl over the pan of water. Add the chocolate, and stir until it has melted. Cover and leave to cool until the mixture is of a piping consistency. Spoon into a pastry bag fitted with a large star tip and pipe in whirls into paper candy cases. Leave to set.

Note If the mixture becomes too stiff to pipe, it should be re-heated over a pan of hot water.

CHOCOLATE AND ORANGE FUDGE

Makes 36

1 lb granulated sugar
½ cup milk
4oz compound chocolate, broken into small pieces
½ cup butter
grated rind and juice of 1 orange

Well butter a shallow 7 inch square pan. Put all the ingredients in a large pan, and stir over low heat until the sugar has dissolved. Bring to the boil and boil rapidly to 240°F on a candy thermometer (soft ball stage). Stir from time to time to prevent it from burning. Remove from the heat and leave to cool for about 3 minutes. Beat rapidly until thick and creamy. Pour immediately into the prepared pan. When it is beginning to set, mark the fudge into squares with a sharp knife. When cold, cut into squares.

CHOCOLATE POPCORN

1 cup popping corn
½ cup butter
4 tablespoons instant chocolate milk mix
or 1 package instant chocolate dessert mix

Pop the corn following the directions on the package. Melt the butter in a pan and stir into the corn, then sprinkle with the chocolate mix, and toss together lightly.

Variation
Add ½ teaspoon ground cinnamon to the chocolate mix.

WALNUT MOCHA FUDGE

Makes 36

2 cups soft brown sugar
¾ cup canned evaporated milk
½ cup water
¼ cup butter
1 tablespoon instant coffee granules
4oz semisweet chocolate **or** compound chocolate, broken into small pieces
½ cup walnuts, chopped

Well butter a shallow 7 inch square pan. Put the sugar, milk, water, butter and coffee in a large pan. Stir over low heat until the sugar has dissolved. Bring to the boil and boil rapidly to 240°F on a candy thermometer (soft ball stage). Stir from time to time to prevent it from burning. Remove from the heat and stir in the chocolate until melted. Add the walnuts, and beat until the mixture is thick and creamy. Pour immediately into the prepared tin. When it is beginning to set, mark into squares with a sharp knife. When cold, cut into squares.

CHOCOLATE TOFFEE

Makes 36

2 cups granulated sugar
½ cup butter
½ cup water
¼ teaspoon cream of tartar (optional)
4 oz semisweet chocolate **or** compound chocolate,
broken into small pieces

Butter a shallow 7 inch square cake pan. Put the sugar, butter, water and cream of tartar, if using, in a large pan. Stir over low heat until the sugar has dissolved. Bring to the boil and cook without stirring to 280°F on a candy thermometer (soft crack stage). After 250°F is reached (hard ball stage), reduce the heat and cook very slowly up to the required temperature. Remove from the heat and add the chocolate. Stir gently until melted, then pour immediately into the prepared pan. When beginning to set, mark into squares with a sharp knife. Leave to set, and cut into squares when cold.

Note These toffees can be wrapped individually in waxed papers for storing.

CHOCOLATE PEPPERMINT CREAMS

Makes about 48

1 egg white
¼ teaspoon peppermint extract
a few drops green food coloring (optional)
3 cups confectioners sugar, sifted
4 oz semisweet **or** milk chocolate,
broken into small pieces

Put the egg white, extract and coloring, if used, in a mixing bowl and beat lightly. Beat in the confectioners sugar gradually to make a firm paste (the exact amount of sugar will depend on the size of the egg). Place on a surface lightly dusted with confectioners sugar and knead until smooth. Roll out, using confectioners sugar to prevent it from sticking, to a thickness of about ¼ inch. Stamp out circles, using a 1½ inch cutter and place on a cookie sheet lined with wax paper. Mark each one with the prongs of a fork. Leave in a warm place overnight to dry out.

Melt the chocolate (page 11). Dip each peppermint cream in the chocolate so that only half is coated. Shake off any excess chocolate and place on buttered wax paper or foil. Leave to set.

MINT CRISPS

Makes about 30

4 tablespoons water
4 tablespoons granulated sugar
1 teaspoon peppermint extract
8 oz semisweet chocolate, broken into small pieces

Well butter a piece of wax paper. Put the water and sugar into a small, heavy-based pan. Stir over low heat until the sugar has dissolved, then boil rapidly to 280°F on a candy thermometer (soft crack stage). Remove from the heat and stir in the extract. Pour evenly over the wax paper and leave to set. When the mixture is quite firm, either break up into small pieces with a rolling-pin or chop finely in a food processor; the pieces should resemble coarse breadcrumbs.

Melt the chocolate (page 11), then remove from the heat and stir in the peppermint pieces. Put teaspoonfuls of the mixture on sheets of buttered wax paper, spread into circles about 1 inch in diameter, and leave to set.

FRUIT AND NUT CLUSTERS

Makes 24–28

4 oz semisweet chocolate, broken into small pieces
2 tablespoons honey
½ cup mixed dried fruit
¼ cup nuts, chopped, eg almonds, hazelnuts
or brazils
grated rind of ½ orange

DECORATION
candied cherries

Melt the chocolate with the honey (page 11). Stir in the dried fruit, nuts and orange rind until well coated in the chocolate. Drop teaspoonfuls of the mixture on to buttered wax paper, or into paper candy cases. Press a small piece of candied cherry on the top of each cluster and leave to set.

Variations
Use milk chocolate instead of semisweet chocolate.
Different colored candied cherries look very attractive.

STUFFED DATES

Makes about 24

1 lb fresh dates
3 oz semisweet chocolate, broken into small pieces
¼ cup butter
1 tablespoon ground almonds
1 egg yolk
1 tablespoon Grand Marnier **or** other
orange liqueur
grated rind of 1 small orange

COATING

6 oz semisweet chocolate, broken into small pieces
1 tablespoon vegetable shortening

Using a sharp knife, make a slit down the side of each date and remove the seed. Pull off the hard remains of the stem. Melt the chocolate (page 11) and remove from the heat. Cream the butter. Beat in the ground almonds, then the egg yolk. Beat in the Grand Marnier, orange rind and finally the chocolate. Mix well, then chill in a refrigerator for about 10 minutes, or until the mixture is firm enough to pipe.

Fill a small pastry bag fitted with a small plain tip about ¼ inch wide with the mixture, or put it into a heavy-gauge polythene bag, work it down to one corner and snip off the corner with shears. Holding the dates between the thumb and forefinger, press them open and pipe the filling into the center. Chill in a refrigerator for about 15 minutes.

To make the coating, melt the chocolate with the vegetable shortening (page 11), and pour into a narrow deep glass or cup. Taking one date at a time, skewer one end with a toothpick and dip into the melted chocolate. Allow the excess chocolate to drip off, then place on a piece of foil and use a second stick to push the date off the dipping stick. Leave to set.

Variation

Fill the dates with half of the mixture and then pipe the remainder on to some buttered wax paper, making small 'blobs' the size of a large marble. Chill for about 15 minutes, then dip into melted chocolate and leave to set.

CHRISTMAS FRUIT BALLS

Makes 20

1 dessert apple, peeled
1 tablespoon lemon juice
½ cup dried apricots
½ cup golden raisins
2 tablespoons blanched almonds
6 oz bittersweet chocolate, broken into small pieces

Chop the apple finely. Place in a mixing bowl and pour over the lemon juice. Chop the apricots, golden raisins and almonds finely, add to the apple and mix together well. Using your hands, squeeze the fruit mixture together and shape into 20 small balls.

Melt the chocolate (page 11). Spear the fruit balls with a fork and coat them with melted chocolate. Place on buttered waxed paper and leave to dry. Put in paper candy cases or wrap in small squares of foil and tie with lengths of fine ribbon to hang on the Christmas tree.

SAUCES AND DRINKS

Chocolate sauce is the perfect accompaniment for ice cream and numerous other desserts, both hot and cold. Use any of the recipes in this chapter and see how easy it is to transform a simple dessert into something quite special.

If you want to make a chocolate sauce which is not too sweet, use unsweetened chocolate as this produces a really excellent rich sauce. Try any of these recipes using unsweetened chocolate, and add just a very little extra sugar.

Chocolate milk shakes are always popular and for these you can use either a commerical syrup or instant chocolate milk mix. The home-made syrup on page 79 is, however, extremely useful as it keeps in a refrigerator for weeks.

RICH CHOCOLATE SAUCE (1)

Serves 4–6

1 heaping tablespoon cocoa powder
¾ cup canned evaporated milk
3 oz semisweet chocolate, broken into small pieces

Whisk together the cocoa and evaporated milk in a small pan. Put over low heat and bring to boiling point. Remove from the heat and stir in the chocolate. Return to low heat and continue stirring until the chocolate has melted.

Note If serving this sauce cold, add about 3 tablespoons light cream to keep it at a pouring consistency.

CHOCOLATE AND ORANGE SAUCE

Serves 4–6

½ cup fresh orange juice
grated rind of 1 orange
2 tablespoons butter
1 cup milk chocolate chips

Heat the orange juice and rind, and the butter in a small pan and, when the butter has melted, bring to boiling point. Remove from the heat, stir in the chocolate and return to the heat, stirring all the time. When the chocolate has melted, boil for about 1 minute.

Note Orange juice from a carton can be used instead of the fresh orange juice and rind, but this does not give such a strong orange flavor to the sauce.

RICH CHOCOLATE SAUCE (2)

Serves 6–8

½ cup butter
½ cup caster sugar
a pinch of salt
2 tablespoons dark rum
½ cup cocoa powder
½ cup heavy cream
1 teaspoon vanilla extract

Melt the butter in a small pan. Stir in the sugar, salt, rum and the cocoa. Mix well over low heat. Add the cream and bring to the boil. Simmer very gently for 5 minutes. Remove from the heat and add the vanilla extract. Serve hot or cold.

CHARLOTTE'S PEPPERMINT SAUCE

Serves 4–6

3 oz chocolate-covered peppermint creams
½ cup light cream

Break each chocolate in half and melt in a bowl over a pan of hot water. Remove from the heat and gradually stir in the cream. Serve warm or cold.
Serve with ice cream.

BITTER FUDGE SAUCE

Serves 4–6

⅓ cup butter
2 oz unsweetened chocolate
¼ cup granulated sugar
½ cup light cream

Put all the ingredients into a small pan. Put over a gentle heat, stirring frequently until the butter and chocolate have melted. Bring to the boil for about 1 minute, stirring all the time, until a smooth, thick sauce is obtained. Serve hot.

Variation
Flavor the sauce with rum, brandy or any liqueur. Add after the sauce has boiled.

CHOCOLATE FUDGE SAUCE

Serves 4–6

¼ cup unsalted butter
½ cup milk
2 tablespoons caster sugar
4 oz semisweet chocolate, broken into small pieces

Put the butter, milk and sugar into a small pan and bring to the boil. Remove from the heat and add the chocolate. Stir until the chocolate has melted, then return to the heat and boil rapidly for 2 minutes.

Note If serving this sauce cold, add about 3 tablespoons light cream to keep it at a pouring consistency.

CARIBBEAN CHOCOLATE

Serves 1

1 cup milk
1½ tablespoons instant chocolate milk mix
a good pinch of ground nutmeg
a good pinch of ground allspice
a good pinch of ground cinnamon
1 tablespoon whipped cream
extra instant chocolate milk mix

Put the milk, chocolate and spices into a pan and bring to the boil. Remove from the heat, beat well and pour into a mug. Top with the whipped cream and sprinkle with a little extra chocolate milk mix.

A Selection of Drinks
Coffee Choco (page 78), Crunchy Peppermint Milk Shake (page 78) Caribbean Chocolate **and** *Iced Chocolate (page 78)*

RUM TODDY

Serves 1

½oz semisweet chocolate, broken into pieces
½ cup milk
1 tablespoon dark rum
1 heaping teaspoon whipped cream
a little grated nutmeg

Put the chocolate and milk into a small pan and bring to the boil, stirring once or twice. Remove from the heat and beat in the rum. Pour into a small cup or glass. Top with the cream and sprinkle with the nutmeg.

ICED CHOCOLATE

Serves 4

1 cup milk
½ cup light cream
3 tablespoons Chocolate Syrup
(page 79)
8 ice cubes (approx)

Beat together the milk, cream and syrup. Put the ice cubes into a jug, pour over the chocolate, and serve.

Variation
Top with small scoops of ice cream.

COFFEE CHOCO

Serves 4

1½ cups milk
1½ cups water
1½ tablespoons instant coffee granules
1 tablespoon instant chocolate milk mix
4 chocolate flake bars

Heat the milk and water to just below boiling point. Blend in the coffee and chocolate mix, and mix well. Pour into glasses and put a chocolate flake into each glass.

CRUNCHY PEPPERMINT MILK SHAKE

Serves 1

2 tablespoons semisweet chocolate bits
3 tablespoons chocolate ice cream
½ cup cold milk
¼ teaspoon peppermint extract

Put the chocolate bits into a blender or food processor and chop finely. Add all the remaining ingredients and blend for a further 30 seconds until well mixed and frothy. Serve at once.

QUICKIE MILK SHAKE

Serves 1

3 heaping tablespoons vanilla ice cream
2 tablespoons instant chocolate milk mix
$\frac{1}{2}$ cup milk

Blend all the ingredients in a blender or food processor for about 30 seconds. Serve immediately.

CHOCOLATE SYRUP

$1\frac{1}{2}$ cups soft brown sugar
1 cup cocoa powder
$\frac{1}{4}$ teaspoon salt
1 cup water
2 teaspoons vanilla extract

Put all the ingredients, except the vanilla extract, into a pan, mix well and bring to the boil. Cook gently for 5 minutes, stirring frequently. Remove from the heat, leave to cool, then stir in the vanilla extract. Cover and chill in a refrigerator until required.

Use as a base for milk shakes, or pour over ice cream as a sauce, and thin with a little milk.

INDEX OF RECIPES